GIRL ABOUT TOWN

GIRL ABOUT TOWN

A City Girl's Guide to Life

Cathay Che and Rachel Pask

PERIGEE

Perigee Book
Published by The Berkley Publishing Group
A division of Penguin Group (USA) Inc.
375 Hudson Street
New York, New York 10014

Conceived and produced by
Elwin Street Limited
79 St John Street
London EC1M 4NR
www.elwinstreet.com

Perigee trade paperback edition: March 2005
Visit our website at www.penguin.com

This book has been cataloged by the Library of Congress.
ISBN 0-399-53098-3

Printed in Singapore
10 9 8 7 6 5 4 3 2 1

Designer: Mark Jonathan Latter

Illustrator: Veronica Palmieri

Contents

So, you're moving to a big city. You don't know a soul. In fact, you have no idea where you're going to work, who you'll hang out with, or even where you'll be sipping your favorite cocktails come Saturday night.

But you know you have to go—to put yourself on the path to amazing success and adventure. Just how you're going to find your way around and figure it all out is a bit of a mystery right now, but you're bright, young, and confident (well, most of the time). Every new chick in the metropolis finds taking those first steps onto the fantastic fast-paced streets a little daunting at first, but it won't be long before you're soaking up the glamorous urban lifestyle, and strutting around like a native in the heart of the city.

And for the things that take a little know-how to put into place, help is at hand. From making your pad look like it's straight out the pages of *Lucky* magazine, to knowing where to pick up the best designer duds at discount prices, this book is your bible. Don't feel like you have to read it from beginning to end—dip in and out, and pick the chapter that is relevant to what you're going through. You're smart—so it won't take long to get the hang of it.

URBAN LIVING

How to find the perfect apartment

The city is a huge and unwieldy maze of people, places, and things. In somewhere so big and sometimes entirely overwhelming, it's essential you find a place to call home. It can be difficult to know whether to look uptown or downtown, east end or west, to rent or to buy, to find a roommate or to live alone. If searching for your own place feels a bit daunting, take inspiration from Madonna's boldness.

After dropping out of college, Madge moved to New York to be a dancer with just $35 in her pocket (and a furious father at the back of her mind). She stepped off the plane and into a taxi, telling the driver, "Take me to the center of everything." The next thing she knew, she was standing in Times Square. The cab ride cost her half the money she had, but almost immediately she was feeding off the city's phenomenal energy. She also was lucky enough to meet kind strangers who took her in until she found a place of her own. And look how it worked out for her!

Kind strangers aside (which are obviously a bad idea), simply launching out on your own will be the best thing you've ever done. There will be lessons to learn, but these will become your own personal folklore—part of the amazing story of your life.

Before you can start looking for a place, you need to decide which area of the city you want to live in. Hoping for somewhere huge, fabulous, and in the center of town is probably a little unrealistic. Try to narrow down your priorities. Would you rather have a big place in an up-and-coming area, or a smaller apartment somewhere more chic? Take a day to wander around the places that appeal to you the most to get a real feel for them. Pick up a couple of local papers from the newsstands; they will give some indication of what kind of people live in which

> When I moved to New York, I shared a three-bedroom apartment with three friends. Unfortunately one guy stopped paying his rent after six months and we had the choice of either dividing it up between the rest of us, or being evicted. To make matters worse, my parents guaranteed the lease, which meant that if we didn't pay, the landlord would go after them for the money. I'd recommend making sure the lease says you are only responsible for your room's rent, not for the rent of the whole apartment. That way if someone doesn't pay, it's the landlord's problem, not yours. L U C Y , 2 8

neighborhoods, and what goes on there. Visit the area during the day and at night—it might feel quite different, and you will want to be comfortable walking around in the dark. Chances are, you'll probably know someone in the city, so check out where they live and see if that neighborhood suits you. Even if you begin to live in one area, and move on after a couple of months when you have found your feet, it is great to have a place to call your own.

If you have moved abroad, you may find there are some parts of the city that are popular with your fellow countrymen. How do you find them? Well, if you're British you might head for the city's best-known Brit pub. If you're French, you might look for a French film series at the local university. If you're feeling a bit homesick, or simply missing the food or a friendly accent, seeking out peers can be comforting.

It is important not to limit yourself strictly to any one area because location can have a massive impact on the price of your rent. To rent a room in an apartment share in Manhattan's West Village will cost you upwards of $1500 a month, while across town in the East Village you could find something similar for only $1000 a month. If you're looking for a property with friends, try websites to get an idea of rental rates. There are also websites that advertise shares if you have come to the city without your own roommates. Naturally some parts of the city will be more developed and desirable than others, and prices will vary accordingly.

If you already know where you are going to be working, buy a comprehensive street directory of your city from a bookshop. Then it will be easy to work out exactly how far you will be from work, and to see what kind of transportation is available for your daily commute. Even if you don't have a job yet, you probably

have a good idea about where you'll want to be working, so bear in mind that living somewhere convenient to where you work will save you money as well as time.

How long it will take you to get to key places like your job is a really important factor to consider. Sometimes a two-mile journey can take the same amount of time as a ten-mile trip because of the different types of transportation available. Most trains and subways have websites where you can plan your journey—they give the times of trains and information on how long it will take to get to your destination. This should help you decide exactly how far in, or out, you want to base yourself. And once you've narrowed down where you want to live, at least you know where to start looking.

In the meantime, you're probably couch surfing at someone else's place. While this can be fun, it can also go horribly wrong. Whether you're staying with friends, family, or friends of family, there are a few things you should bear in mind to ensure it is a positive experience.

houseguest rules

It's almost a rite of passage when you're moving to the big city to crash on someone's couch while you settle in and get your bearings. Following are a few tips to make this transition as painless as possible:

• Some people are happy to let you freeload, but you should offer to help out with household costs and contribute to the bills while you are there. Take the initiative and help out with cleaning up too.

• If you are sleeping in the living room, try and clear your things early in the morning so everyone else in the house or apartment is able to use it. In the evening, remember that no one should have to go to bed early just because you want to.

• Buying flowers, household supplies (such as toilet paper, soap, and garbage bags) and cooking a few good meals for everyone will help extend your welcome and ensure a pleasant experience.

Apartment vs. house

It's really important to consider what you want before you head out there to look for it. Are you looking for a house or an apartment to share? It's probably best if you don't even dream about luxuries such as two bathrooms and large well-appointed kitchens, and it wouldn't hurt to re-adjust your idea of the importance of the size of your bedroom. When you move to the city, you will discover that space has its price. Don't worry, though, you will soon have all the space you need at your local café and pub, and a bigger yard than you ever had growing up in the park nearby.

If you are considering an apartment, would you like a conversion—a house that has been split into apartments—so there will be big windows, lots of light, and high ceilings? Or would you feel more at home in an apartment building where the accommodation will be fairly new and well laid out—but you're more likely to hear everything going on with the couple next door? Houses often come with a larger number of rooms and this means you'll be sharing with and meeting more people, but it may be noisier, and more crowded. Do you think you can cope with sharing one kitchen and one bathroom with four other people?

Where to look

In order to find a property, you could start by dropping in on a real estate agent. They are usually located on most main streets. This will give you a good idea of what the market prices are in the different areas, but remember that everyone else in your situation is probably looking at these same places, as real estate agents are the most obvious first stop. Next, pick up the local papers—especially the alternative weekly papers that are often given out free in cafés and artist spaces. The best listings in the major papers often come out on Saturdays and Sundays. Keep your ear to the ground. As you make new acquaintances, ask them if they know of anyone looking for a roommate. Cities are held together by connections and networking. Check bulletin boards at universities. You can often hear about great places through friends, friends of friends, or even by just striking up a friendly conversation at a party or after a show. People are often more comfortable rooming with or renting to people they have some kind of personal connection with. Would you rather take your chances on a complete stranger who could turn out to put rat poison in your pickles, or someone who was recommended by someone you know?

You can also do a lot of your searching online—many realtors have their properties on their websites and you can go on a "virtual tour." Always note whether the number to call to inquire about a place is a real estate agent, a landlord, or the person renting the place. If you don't deal with an agent, you'll save yourself the finder's fees charged by many agents—these fees can be up to one month's rent—but agents generally make the process a lot smoother and have nicer properties to show.

quick fix After seeing a whole bunch of apartments you realize that the first one you turned down was actually a good deal. Now what? Get on the phone right away. This is business—not personal. Whether it's a private landlord or an agent, their only interest is in renting that property, so don't be embarrassed, and don't feel like you have to give any explanation.

Things to ask

First and foremost you need to find out how much the rent is and whether bills (usually gas and electric, sometimes a shared phone line or cable TV) are included. Most often they're not. How much is the deposit, and will the landlord require first and last month's rent in advance? Will you be on the lease? The lease specifies the

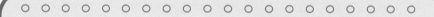

before you sign

- Check how much the rent is, when it is due, and how your landlord expects it to be paid.

- Are the bills included? If not, what do they run to on average and to whom are they paid?

- Read through the lease carefully and ask questions about anything you're unsure of.

- How long is the lease for and how much is the deposit?

- Are you allowed to have roommates?

- Does the property require any major repair work? Confirm when this will be carried out and request a reduced rate in your rent in the meantime.

- Are you allowed to have pets?

- Complete and sign an inventory if the apartment is furnished, or a condition report if it is unfurnished.

- Never rely on verbal agreements. All conditions of the tenancy should be written into the lease or put into a contract you make with your new roommates.

amount of time you agree to rent a property at the advertised rent—a year is pretty standard. Be careful of signing a lease for longer than a year, because if you want to leave you may be liable to pay rent for the rest of the agreed time—or at the very least, you will lose your deposit.

If you're not sure about the terms of the lease, seek advice from a tenant's rights organization. Just enter "tenant's rights" plus the name of your city, for example "tenant's rights Chicago," in an Internet search and a list of resources will come up. And of course, if you are going to be living with other people, arrange a meeting, and make sure you like them as much as you like the place. You don't want to be stuck in a fabulous pad with hellish roommates.

Securing the right space

Even though the rent might seem astronomical, if you like somewhere you'll have to move fast. For starters, you need to make sure you have cash to put down as a deposit—normally the equivalent of the first month's rent—plus pay your first month's rent upfront. The idea behind this is that if you fail to pay the rent or cause any damage to the place, the landlord can use this money to fix things. Some landlords will also require the last month's rent.

Before moving in, ask your landlord for an inventory of all the items in the apartment, and give it a quick check through to make sure there's nothing missing. If your new place is unfurnished, just make note of anything in the space that isn't working properly, such as lights that don't turn on, leaking faucets, and broken cabinets, or anything that looks damaged, such as broken window panes, or holes in the wall. This is to establish that you didn't break or damage it. Give your landlord a list of things you want repaired—it's your right to move into a fully functioning space.

Before you start putting up mirrors, pictures, or bathroom cabinets, ask your landlord whether it's OK—it sounds petty, but you could risk losing your deposit by leaving marks on the walls, and it's not worth running the risk. Additionally, if your room needs a coat of paint, ask your landlord to pay for the materials and offer to do it yourself—the fastest and easiest way by far. If you decide to paint your walls any color other than white, you may be required to paint it back to white before you vacate.

It is usually the tenant's responsibility to pay for the gas and electricity, and it's up to the landlord to ensure that all appliances and installations are kept in safe, working order. It will be up to you whether you want to have a phone line, cable TV, or a high-speed Internet connection in your new place, but when you open accounts in your name, make sure there isn't an outstanding balance from the previous tenant being transferred to you. And it is up to you to take out renter's insurance for any of your personal belongings. If you have roommates, try to put as many bills as you can in your own name. If you have some shared bills, make sure you establish right away when and how they will be paid.

Living in harmony

The chances are, when you move into a shared place, there will be people who have already been living there for months, if not years. People in these situations are used to transition, so you shouldn't feel like the newbie for too long. To get off on the right foot, find out if there are any house-rules. Maybe everyone is expected to clean up after themselves and buy their own groceries? Or maybe all the household chores are assigned, or certain household items, such as milk, coffee, and bottled water are shared, and paid for out of a central fund? If you find out how things run as soon as you move in, you will avoid treading on any toes.

Even if it makes waves at first, it's probably better to opt out of using the communal landline phone—if there is one. Get yourself a cell phone with 1000 plus minutes—there are some great deals to be found on the web and at cell phone retailers. Then you won't have to rely on others passing on messages, spend time waiting to use the phone, and you will avoid the monthly trauma of deciphering the phone bill to work out who owes what.

On the other hand, it probably does make sense to split cable TV and high-speed Internet access if it's already installed and you can use it equally with your roommates.

Avoiding roommate hell

Think carefully about what kind of people you want to live with. At a very basic level, roommates don't have to be people you'd be friends with, but people you can live comfortably with.

If you work regular business hours, maybe you want everyone else to have 9–5 jobs too, so that weeknights will be quiet and there will be a bit of noise and merriment on the weekends. Alternately, if people are working different hours, that may mean you can count on some alone time in the house or apartment each day. But you will need to make sure you're quiet when others are sleeping, and likewise they should offer you the same courtesy.

the roommate interview: interviewee

The roommate interview is a slightly stressful scenario, whether you are the one deciding on someone or being decided upon. What you have to remember is that both parties are simply trying to figure out if you are likely to be compatible roommates. This is not *American Idol* where you're being judged on your talent or the way you wear your hair, so try not to get defensive or put on too much of a show. There's no point pretending to be someone you're not, because just like the roommates on MTV's *The Real World*, you won't be able to keep being polite 24/7—so you might as well start by being real.

Here are some of the things you might want to ask if you are being interviewed as a potential roommate:

- Are there any house-rules? Are they negotiable?

- How much are the household bills on average? Who actually has to write the check or make the call to pay them? When are they due?

- What are you looking for in a roommate?

- Do you mind . . . (insert any potential problem areas).

- Why did the last roommate leave?

- Is it more of a party-house or a quiet-house?

- Do you allow overnight guests? Are there any limits on how long a guest can stay?

- How will house problems or decisions be handled? Is there one person who deals with the landlord or the super?

the roommate interview: interviewer

You've found a great place to live. It's in a great neighborhood, it has fantastic lighting, a great bathroom and kitchen—in fact is is everything you want in an apartment—but it is way beyond what you can afford. There is an easy solution. You need to find roommates to share it with. The first thing to do is place an ad in the paper or on the Internet. Think about the type of people you want to live with. Are you looking for people who are going to be financially responsible but not necessarily people you'd spend any extra time with, or are you wanting to live with people who you get along with and might end up being your friends?

As well as running the house-rules past your potential new roommates, here are some of the things you might want to ask:

- Do you smoke?
- Do you have a boyfriend/girlfriend? Will he/she be staying over?
- Why are you moving—where have you come from?
- What kind of music are you into?
- Are you a homebody or do you prefer going out?
- What are your pet peeves?
- Are you an early riser or a night owl?
- Are you fastidiously tidy, messy, or somewhere in between?
- Are you financially responsible?
- Do you have any pets?

Finding really fabulous roommates

Finding people to share with you is even harder than finding a room or apartment for yourself. What you need is not really fantastic new friends, although of course that would be a great start, but people you can trust to look after themselves and your shared home. You want to avoid people who will constantly turn to you to sort out any problems, whether they are short on cash for the bills or household repairs, or suffering from a broken heart.

Where do you find someone to live with? Send an email around at work. Put a sign up in your gym. Talk to acquaintances who might know someone looking to save a bit of cash by sharing a house or an apartment. It's worth mentioning it to your landlord too. If he or she rents a few properties, they might be in touch with people who are looking for roommates. Try roommate websites also and of course, look through the listings in your local papers.

When you think you've found a potential roomie, talk about what you expect sharing to be like. Focus on these issues: Will you split the bills down the middle? Will you share decisions on the decor? Will you take it in turns to clean? Are you happy to go out if they want a friend over and vice versa? Do they get up early while you get up late? Discuss pet peeves now, rather than when they're sitting on the sofa firing toenail clippings all over the carpet.

Just because you wouldn't go clubbing with someone doesn't mean they won't be a good person to live with. In fact, sometimes moving in with your best friend is the fastest way to kill a friendship. Once you've found the gal or guy for the job, do everything you can to be a good person to live with and your home life should blossom.

Dealing with monster landlords

In theory, landlords should never be monsters unless you haven't paid your rent. And then you really can't blame them for being hard on you. However if they don't send someone round to fix the boiler when it's been broken for two weeks, or they appear every few days just to check how things are, then it's time for a discussion. When general repairs are being ignored, call often, keeping a record of your calls, the content of your conversations, dates, and times. Explain the problem clearly and concisely. If persuasion or persistence aren't working, as a last resort you may decide to warn your landlord that unless they carry out the repairs, you will have them done and deduct the cost from future payments of rent. Get at least two estimates first and send these to the landlord in advance to show that it is a reasonable price.

If your landlord keeps magically appearing to "check in," explain that you expect to receive a phone call first. Although landlords frequently keep keys to the properties they rent out (and this can be a good thing for you if you should lock yourself out one day), the law does not allow them right of entry unless this is specifically stated in the tenancy agreement. A landlord might arrange to come round to see what repairs need to be done, but otherwise, he or she has no more right to enter your house than a stranger. If your landlord's behavior makes you feel uncomfortable, politely make your feelings clear.

The period of tenancy—how long you have agreed to stay in a property—is legally binding on both sides. Your period of tenancy is spelled out in your lease. While you are living at the property you have to go along with all the conditions set out in the lease, so make sure you read it carefully before you sign. If you are in a share and your names all appear on the lease, then you are all jointly liable for the full payment of the rent during the period of the lease. If one person decides to leave, everyone will have to cough up to cover the extra share of the rent. This is one big reason why it's good to be selective when choosing new roommates.

Landlords are obligated to keep the structure and exterior of their property (including drains, gutters, and external pipes) in good working condition. They have to ensure that the water, gas, electricity, sinks, baths, and toilets work properly. It is the landlord's responsibility to ensure the property is structurally sound, and there is adequate lighting, heating, water, and ventilation. They must also install a smoke detector and removable window guards for windows leading out to a fire escape stairwell. Any furniture supplied, such as beds and sofas, should be fire resistant and marked with a label to show they comply with the regulations. Landlords cannot remove or restrict any of the utilities, prevent you from having visitors, or tamper with your mail or possessions. Pets, however, are at their discretion—best to ask in advance.

If you are renting a property and have a lease, you can't be forced to move out of a place without a court order and just cause. You have rights and you can get help from a tenant's rights organization in your city. If you have paid all rent due at the end of your lease and your landlord is making false claims about the condition of the property and refusing to return your deposit, you may want to seek a compromise simply to avoid a costly court case. A strongly worded letter to the landlord from a lawyer should do the trick, disputing the damage and proposing a lower figure. Talk to a tenant's rights organization to find a housing lawyer in your area.

If your landlord turns out to be a menace in any way, it will be stressful and scary, but a housing lawyer will tell you that this kind of thing happens all too often—just steel yourself and don't give in to threats and intimidation—the law is on your side.

Home sweet home

It might not be a palace, but a few cosmetic repairs and a little decorative camouflage can go a long way in covering up uneven plastering, worn furniture, and old carpets. From the start, aim for an uncluttered look. This will give any room style, give the impression that the room is clean, and you can cleverly disguise a lack of homey stuff and trinkets by making the things you have a real feature.

Getting your bedroom how you want it is really important in order to make sure you feel comfortable and at home. Before you move your things in, make a list of the five things you will spend the most time doing in your bedroom. These might include sleeping, dressing, watching TV, working on your computer and, on occasion, entertaining. Then think about what you might want to have in your room to support those activities—you may even want to draw a floor plan and cut out pieces of paper to scale to represent everything you want to fit in there, such as a bed, desk, and sofa. Then move them around to see where things might go before you

quick fix With people moving in and out so rapidly in a shared house and a merry-go-round of their friends and lovers frequently dropping by, you're a bit worried about the safety of all your stuff. Ask your landlord for the key to your door. If there isn't one, invest in a simple padlock. And keep jewelry, your laptop, or other valuables hidden from plain sight someplace not so obvious, such as under your pillow, in a dresser drawer under clothes, or in a ziplock inside a Kleenex box under a few layers of tissues.

actually start pushing furniture around. Your bedroom is the one place you can retreat to, so try to make it as soothing and uncluttered as possible. It is also the place where you dream and get ready to face the day, so it should feel optimistic and ordered so you can start the day on a positive note.

Hang muslin drapes above your bed to give a feeling of intimacy—it's cheap and easy to do, and will double up as a mosquito protector in the summer! Invest in some funky rugs from the cheaper furniture and soft furnishing stores—you can easily take these with you when you move. Place one beside your bed so that when you get up in the morning you'll feel something nice between your toes.

Buy some storage boxes to stash your out-of-season clothes under your bed, rather than having them clutter up your closet all year round. Keep your shoes in their boxes, take a Polaroid of each pair, and stick it on the front of the correct box—that way they will be kept in good condition, be easy to find, and your shoe display becomes a design feature. Get a laundry basket so that your dirty clothes are not strewn all over the floor. Splurge on some floor cushions—they look great and are easy to move around when people drop by.

If your room is very small, buy a large mirror and hang it opposite a window to open up the area. If you find one in an antique shop or market, it can be a great way to add character to a room. If the rest of the furniture isn't setting your world on fire, buy some throws to brighten it up. Try hanging sheer white curtains in the window—they will give you some privacy but not take away all the light, so the room feels bigger than it actually is.

In lieu of paintings, you might stretch some printed fabric across a wooden frame and hang it on a blank wall. And if you're really broke, some websites offer free stuff that people want to get rid of such as desks, tables and sofas—all you have to do is go pick it up.

STREET SMARTS

Getting around town

Getting on your feet in a new city is a totally humbling experience. Last week you knew the fastest bus route into town, the cheapest dry cleaners, and the best supermarkets. Today you haven't got a clue about anything in your new environment—you don't even know how not to get ripped-off like a tourist. It's time to do some research so that you look like you've been in the city for years.

Whether it's trains, taxis, buses, or the subway, what to take and when can be confusing. Every city is entirely different. In New York, Washington D.C., San Francisco, Toronto, and Vancouver, many people take public transportation every day to and from work. However, living in Los Angeles, Miami, Honolulu, or a smaller North American city means you'll need a car and will have to drive most places.

Perhaps the first thing you should research about your new city is the public transportation system. If you need a car, you need to figure out if it's going to be more cost-effective for you to buy one and drive it to your new home, or buy one once you arrive. Another popular option is to lease a car. You pay a monthly fee, like paying rent, for use of the car and you have the option to extend your contract from year to year indefinitely. This is cheaper than buying a car outright, but you'll still have to make insurance payments.

Choose a modest car that doesn't draw too much attention but runs well, whatever car you may fantasize about having one day when you are rich and famous. Keep all windows and doors locked when driving around town, and your bags, phone, and any other valuables should be kept out of sight. Don't forget you will most probably have to pay for parking if you need to put your car into a lot, and street parking in many cities is limited to certain hours of the day or subject to steep fines if you overstay your allocated time period. Hopefully, you'll be in a city where having car isn't really necessary, but if you need to drive to work, think about sharing your journey with other people heading in the same direction. Check out the web for carpooling sites.

Public transportation is perhaps the best way to go. It's cheap, provides social interaction, and ensures that one less car is on the road, something the environment will thank you for. In many areas, such as New York City, public transportation is so extensive that not only do most people not own a car, many don't even know how to drive. The subway or metro routes may seem like a chaotic maze at first, but it should be easy enough to get a map of the system before you move. You can do a web search on "public transportation" plus name of your city. Get a sense of the major stops. This may even influence where you decide to live and work. Don't forget to look up the bus, tram, and streetcar routes and times, as well as investigating sea and boat options.

Cycling is also a cost-effective way of getting around a city and will keep you fit at the same time. Try to use bike lanes wherever possible, always remember your helmet and your lights at night, invest in a sturdy D-lock, and leave your bike in a visible place when you lock it up.

> " I was out on the town one night, jostling my way through a crowd of people, when I felt something inside my coat pocket. I immediately checked and realized my purse had gone. At the top of my voice I shouted to my friend, "Someone's just stolen my purse!" There were police around and when we looked on the floor the thief had dropped it in a panic and all my cash was still inside. Now I'm never afraid to use my voice if I need to. ELLIE, 28 "

Staying safe

Whether it's day or night, keep your bag firmly closed and never leave it unattended when you're out. If you're going out to a bar or club, don't take more than a few essentials, including keys, cash/ATM card, cell phone, and lipstick. But if you find yourself having a marathon day where you go from work to your work-out and then on to dinner and dancing, many bars and clubs provide a coat check—for

using ATMs

- Try and get all the cash you need from your bank ATM during the day.
- Avoid using ATMs when you've been drinking.
- If it looks like the ATM has been tampered with, don't use it.
- Check if there is a fee for using the ATM.
- If you see someone suspicious hanging around, walk away and go back later.
- Look around before inserting your card, only take what you need, and don't walk around with bundles of cash in your pockets.
- Don't count your money in full view of strangers.
- Split your cash up so if your purse gets stolen you won't lose everything.
- Memorize your PIN number and never tell anyone your PIN number.

a mere dollar or two, you can stash your bag and not have to worry about it all night. If the worst happens and your phone or cards do get stolen, cancel them immediately and file a report with the police.

When you're in a nightclub or bar, be wary of having your drink spiked. The most widely publicized drug used for this purpose is Rophinol, which is also known as the date-rape drug. It is a prescribed sedative that dissolves quickly in liquid and has no color, odor, or taste. Drink spiking can make you feel sick, drunk, or disorientated. You could have memory loss, and sudden or excessive tiredness, or blackouts. Make sure you get help immediately if you think it's happened to you. Most drugs take effect within 30 minutes and the symptoms may last up to eight hours. If you are with a friend get them to take you home straight away by car or taxi. If you are alone speak to a member of staff and ask them to call a friend. Do not leave the club or bar until they arrive. Don't even think about letting a stranger take you home, however nice or normal they may seem.

bar and club safety

- **Avoid going out for the evening alone.**

- **Alcohol affects your reactions so you'll be less alert. Never accept a drink from someone you don't know.**

- **Drugs can be put in soda too.**

- **Never leave your drink unattended.**

- **Take your drink with you if you're going to the bathroom or to dance, or ask a friend to keep an eye on it.**

- **If your drink has been moved, looks like it has been topped up, or tastes funny, leave it to one side and buy another.**

Making your way home

Before you go out, think about how you're going to get back home. Then factor in that it's going to be late and you might have had a few drinks. If you're going to a nightclub, public transportation services may have stopped running by the time you leave. Make certain you check where the nearest all-night bus stop is located and keep at least three numbers for taxi companies (unless taxis are plentiful on the streets). Make sure you always keep enough money to one side to pay for your fare. You might also arrange to stay with a friend who lives in the center of the city, just in case you get stuck. If you are alone traveling on a late-night bus or train, sit near the driver or conductor and always sit in a busy compartment on the train. If you feel uncomfortable move to another seat or carriage.

You should not wander around at night, particularly if you're alone. When you order a cab from a private service, ask the phone operator for the driver's name. When the cab arrives, check it's the right person, and find out whether he knows your name before you open the door to get in. You can also check his photo ID, which should be displayed on the dashboard. It's best to sit behind the driver, not in the front passenger seat. Whatever you do, never ever get in an unlicensed taxi. As an extra safety measure, either arrange to call a friend when you arrive safely at home, or send your friend or roommates a text message to say where you are and when you expect to be home.

If you can't avoid walking around at night, stick to well-lit routes away from potential danger spots such as dark alleys, empty parking lots, parks, and shortcuts. Walk confidently, hold your head high, and try to look as if you know where you are going. Listening to a personal stereo or chatting on your cell phone is a bad idea because it can make you unaware of your surroundings.

Turn around and make eye-contact with anyone you think is following you. Most attackers rely on the element of surprise and often won't choose someone they are not sure they can overpower. If you see a crowd coming toward you, cross the street and walk on the other side. If you feel threatened, don't be afraid to ask for help from passers-by, or go into a place where there are other people, such as a bar or a restaurant. If you are threatened, make as much noise as possible, scream, and set off your personal alarm, available from most good hardware or DIY stores. Remember, you can use reasonable force to defend yourself, so don't be afraid to fight back.

Stay safe at home too. Always lock doors and windows carefully, and invest in deadbolts. Make sure you only buzz people you know into your building if you live in an apartment, and check through the peephole or use a door chain for security at your apartment door.

Health 101

When you move to the city you'll need to find a new doctor and a dentist, preferably before you get sick or break a tooth and need one urgently.

If you are a Canadian citizen or a landed immigrant moving to a city in Canada, your provincial health system has you covered. However, regardless of your nationality, if you are moving to a U.S. city, you are on your own.

There is no national medical care program which pays for all health care in the United States. Individuals are responsible for paying for their own medical expenses and these can often be quite high, so many Americans have private health insurance. Your employer should provide you with health insurance with a full-time job. This will cover some of the costs of seeing doctors, dentists, and whatever medications you need. Many plans, however, have a deductible up to $500 that you must pay in full before your insurance starts to cover 80 percent of the additional costs. If you have socialized medicine back home, you may want to schedule an appointment when you visit to have your yearly check-ups. When filling prescription medicines, ask the pharmacist at the drug store to fill your requirements with "generic" brand medication. This is cheaper but just as effective as a branded medicine.

The good news is that many U.S. and Canadian cities have community clinics, usually targeting minority groups, women, or members of the gay and lesbian community, but not exclusive to these groups. These clinics cater to people who are uninsured and offer sliding-scale fees. For a full list of these clinics, do a web search on "community clinics" plus your city. And of course, if you are looking for low-cost gynecological care or contraception, there is an extensive network of Planned Parenthood clinics all over North America. Even at a clinic, you will still be expected to pay what you can, usually figured out in relation to your annual income.

Stocking your pantry

To stay healthy you have to eat well. But not all supermarkets are created equal. There are top-of-the-line chains, and low-rent chains, organic supermarkets, and health food stores, as well as local produce sold at farmer's markets—these can sometimes provide the best options in terms of fresh fruits and vegetables at moderate prices. Produce tends to be the key when looking at a supermarket—the quality and prices in this department tend to reflect the standard of the rest of the store. And in many cities, it is actually cheaper to go to an inexpensive restaurant and pay $8 for a fresh fish, green salad, and rice pilaf meal than it would be to buy the ingredients at a city supermarket and make the same thing at home.

Bulk shopping emporiums such as Costco, and cheap chain convenience stores such as Wal-Mart and Target, can save you a significant amount of money on everything from pasta sauce to toothpaste. Of course, most city dwellers don't have the storage space for 20 rolls of toilet paper or a case of Diet Coke, so that's something to consider before buying in bulk. Maybe once you have two or three friends in the city, it would be worth visiting one of these places once every three months, splitting the cost, and dividing up supplies you all need.

If you don't have any transportation and live far away from large superstores, it might be worth having your food delivered to your doorstop for a small fee. If you choose carefully it could work out to be cheaper—and more convenient—than buying from corner stores or independent supermarkets . . . especially if your new apartment requires you to walk up five flights of stairs!

And remember, if you do shop regularly at your local supermarket take a list and never go there when you are hungry. You will be less likely to buy things you don't need if you plan ahead.

LANDING THE PERFECT JOB

Getting a foot in the door

The good news is that simply by moving to the city you have already increased your job possibilities tenfold. Whether you are desperate to work in a hospital, a hotel, or at a magazine, you are at the hub of every industry. Now you just need to know how to turn that fairytale into reality.

It's a cliché, but simply getting inside a company's headquarters can make or break your career. It sounds so simple, but how do you actually begin to edge your way in? There are three different approaches.

First, try to make use of any personal contacts you may have. Did someone from your high school or college or even your hometown move into this industry? Could you trace them via a web search or by looking at the website of the company they work for? What about distant relatives or family friends? If you are keen to learn and obviously impressed by your contact's achievements, they will be flattered and happy to hear from you. After all, they were in the same position once upon a time. And it's too true, many people get started by knowing someone—given how competitive the

quick fix The job of your dreams has been advertised—but you only find out about it the day before. Drop everything. Positions like this don't come up very often. If it means working through the night to get your resume perfect, then do it. The next day you can deliver your application in person to ensure it gets there on time. There is no excuse for submitting a sloppy resume—an employer won't know or care about why it came in that way.

job market is, don't hesitate at all to exploit any advantages you may have. It will still be up to you to prove yourself and show them you can do the job well.

Next, try and set yourself up with some work experience in the industry through an internship. Write to at least 20 different companies explaining in an informed manner exactly why you think what they do is unique and great, and how you would love to spend a few weeks observing, absorbing, and helping in any way possible. Make sure your one-page cover letter is professionally written, and get a friend to check it through for mistakes. Include any relevant experience you already have and the dates when you are available. Attach your resume to the letter and follow up with a phone call two weeks later. Always be pleasant—the company owes you nothing, but they could provide your big break. If you get an internship, it is likely to be unpaid or low paid, so you may have to find another job on the side to actually support yourself. But a good internship in your field is totally worth it for the boost it will give your resume.

Another way to get a foot in the door is to look for an entry-level job, as a secretary or assistant at the company you'd eventually like to be working in. Although you won't be doing exactly what you're interested in, you will be able to pick up valuable advice from colleagues, be among the first to hear about internal jobs, and you can make yourself known as a trustworthy and reliable employee. To find jobs like these talk to your college advisor before you leave or drop in on some recruitment agencies when you arrive. Ask friends to find out if there are any jobs available where they are working—entry-level jobs often go unadvertised because people hear about them by word of mouth. Also local newspapers, magazines, industry trade publications or websites list these positions. And remember, many people start at the bottom and work their way up. It builds character and your pool of skills and experience. It will only take one opportunity to change the direction of your life.

The hottest opportunities

Half the trick to landing your dream job is actually hearing about it in the first place. Like the best items in a sample sale, they're gone before you even know about them. This is why you need to cover every base and approach a job hunt with military precision. Before you move, check industry trade publications and websites in your field to see how many positions are available and how frequently they come up. If you already have a job with an office in the area where you'd like to relocate, find out if it's possible to arrange for an intercompany transfer. You could even apply for positions before you move and set up interviews for once you arrive.

Once in the city, buy the main newspapers and magazines to check out the positions advertised in the back sections. Take time to research companies in your field and log onto company websites. You could even call them to see if they will send you details of internal job opportunities. Post a resume "on spec" to every place you would love to work—by applying in advance you will already be on file whenever a job comes up. It doesn't hurt to let people know you are interested—even if your dream job isn't vacant right now, they might think of you for something else. Talk to people in the industry to find out how they heard about their job. Think about joining a temping agency that supplies cover for holidays and maternity leave in the area you are interested in. Sign up with a headhunter—they can give you advice, and tell you about the positions out there.

The most important thing? Don't just send off your resume to a couple of companies and assume something will work out. You are about to become a little fish in a big pond—be confident, but realistic. You have to do all the legwork, all the chasing, and hit every target you can think of. If you approach 100 people, maybe one will get back to you. But one is all you need.

How to write a killer resume

There's so much advice out there on putting together a resume . . . so before you begin, go to the local library and pick up some books on the subject or look on the Internet. Even if you already have a resume, you should re-write it each time you apply for a job to make it relevant to the position you are applying for. Don't even think about sending out the same standard document each time. It might be easy, but it won't get you where you want to go.

A resume should briefly outline your employment history, qualifications, and education, beginning with the most recent. Don't attach degrees, diplomas, or certificates unless requested, and include the contact details for two references. Make sure you checked with these references first, so they are prepared for the inevitable phone call and have thought about all the glowing things they can say about you.

To tailor your resume to a position you should study the ad thoroughly. What is the employer looking for? What skills do they want? What experience do they require? All of this info should be at the top of your resume and highlighted in your cover letter. Cover letters are designed to complement your resume and provide extra information about you. They don't need to be more than three paragraphs long, but remember how important it is to make a good impression here with polite, concise prose and perfect grammar. If you don't get this right, an employer might not bother to even look at your resume. Make sure you have the name of the person to send it to. In the first paragraph, open by stating which job you are applying for. Explain why you want to work at the company and what you can do for them. In the second paragraph, write why you are suited to the job and flag up two or three key areas of your qualifications or experience. Always end the cover letter positively, with polite thanks and a promise to follow up.

Most companies are flooded with resumes when they advertise a job. Yours may have just ten seconds to impress before it hits the "Yes" or "No" pile. It is unrealistic to expect an employer to read all the way through your resume to find what they are looking for. Try to stick to one page, two at the most. Presentation is key. Find a friend who knows how to use a good design package and get them to knock your resume into sparkling shape so it is clear and easy to read.

o o o o o o o o o

resume checklist

- **Contact details**
- **Qualifications**
- **Employment history**
- **Relevant experience and interests**
- **References**

get the job you really want

- Use your contacts—friends, friends of friends, family friends, and previous employers.
- Network at graduate fairs, work socials, and sales conferences. Be proactive and set up your own networking community through websites.
- Talk to your college career advisor.
- Find out if an intercompany transfer is possible.
- Write to all the companies you're interested in and inquire about internships to gain work experience or entry-level jobs.
- Sign up with a reputable temp agency that might be able to place you in your field.
- Check newspapers, trade press, and free magazines for job opportunities. Look up company websites and educate yourself about all of what they do.

The cardinal sin for young job-seekers? Listing those hobbies and Saturday jobs you did a hundred years ago. Will the fact that you count gardening among your favorite weekend activities and that you once worked as a babysitter really impress someone at an advertising firm? Not likely. Instead, draw up a short list of interests that relate to the job or, better still, get some work experience in a similar company— even a week's experience will be better than none.

Claire Barnard
31 Belmont Street
Allentown, PA 34721
Tel: 615-872-9091

July 15, 2005

Mrs Diana Brown
East Coast Director of Public Relations
Warner Bros
1325 Avenue of the Americas
NY. NY 10001

Dear Mrs Brown,

Ref. 9703 Publicity Assistant
I wish to apply for the above position and enclose my resume as requested in your advertisement in the *New York Times* on July 12, 2005.

Twelve months ago, I started working at the Nestlé headquarters in Allentown, PA as assistant to our marketing director, Ms. Penelope Smith. My main duties include fielding Ms. Smith's calls and emails, keeping her appointment book, arranging catering and lunches, making her travel arrangements, and assisting her with special events and product launches.

I am planning to move to New York City next month, and working in the entertainment industry interests me greatly. I studied French cinema in college and have helped coordinate a small film society here in Allentown. I would be a valuable asset to your company as I am hard-working, creative and really enthusiastic about filmmaking and film promotion.

I am available for interview at your convenience and look forward to hearing from you soon.

Yours sincerely,

Claire Barnard

Resume

Michelle Jenkins
15-605 Prospect Street
Pacific Palisades, CA 90220
Tel: 615-123-9876

SKILLS AND ABILITIES
- Motivating others to share my passion for sports and fitness
- Enjoy being part of a team both in volleyball and for academic work
- Able to work without supervision
- Good at balancing work and study commitments
- Competence in use of all aspects of MS Office XP

ACHIEVEMENTS
- Yoga teacher certification from City Yoga, West Hollywood
- Establishing college yoga class
- Captain of college volleyball team

EDUCATION AND QUALIFICATIONS
2000-2004 BS in Nutritional Science and Toxicology, UC Berkley

Subjects studied included:
Core Science, Exercise Physiology Diet & Nutrition, Human Physiology, Statistics, Anatomy, Safety & Sports Injuries, Sports Anatomy and Physiology, Organisation & Administration, Sports Psychology, Supervision & Management, Kineseology.

1996-2000 Pacific Palisades, High School Diploma

- Captain of high school volleyball team
- Certified Lifeguard
- Coordinated surf clinics for under-privileged kids in the Los Angeles area at Hermosa Beach

EMPLOYMENT
2002 to present. Certified Lifeguard, City and Parks Department, Hermosa Beach, CA. Part time, hours vary from 5 to 15 a week.
- Supervising beach safety
- Water rescue
- Cautioning beachgoers about extreme water/weather conditions
- Keeping detailed log shared with other lifeguards
- Maintaining lifeguard stand

INTERESTS
- Volleyball, pilates, yoga, surfing

REFERENCES
Mr. P. Benn
Director of Parks & Recreation, Hermosa Beach
Tel: 626-246-1000

Prof. S. Cuthberg
UC Berkley Faculty Advisor
Dept of Nutritional Studies & Toxicology
Tel: 415-340-6400

How to dazzle in interviews

Give yourself a pat on the back for starters. You have made it through the hardest part of the selection process and risen to the top of dozens and dozens of resumes. Now it is time for you to shine at the interview. "The best candidate doesn't necessarily get the job: the best interviewee does," warns John Lees, a top career consultant and author.

To feel confident, you need to be well prepared. Research the company, know the role you will be playing, and imagine what kind of questions you will be asked. That way you won't feel like sinking into your turtleneck when a tricky subject comes up— instead you will have an answer at your fingertips. Think about what your future boss is looking for, rather than what you want from them. Frankly speaking, they couldn't care less about what this job could do for you—they want to know what you can do for them. So you need to sell yourself, big time. What makes you so special? Why should you get the job over and above everyone else? Be shameless. Confidence is essential and if you believe in yourself, they will believe in you too.

Don't beat yourself up if you practiced answering some questions in the bathroom mirror the night before and you were about as articulate as Joey Tribianni from *Friends*. When you get to the interview, the adrenalin will be pumping and suddenly you will be fast-thinking, fast-talking, and on fire.

Make sure you have a few questions up your sleeve so you come away fully armed with all the knowledge you need to make a decision about the job. What would your job involve on a daily basis? What are the long-term goals for the position? Will there be any training possibilities? Where could this position lead? Try to drop these questions in at appropriate moments throughout the interview, this will illustrate that you are listening to what they are saying and are eager to find out more.

Tackle the tough questions

Every employer likes to throw a toughie at you. Rise to the challenge and remember, an employer is just as desperate to find the right person for the job as you are to fill it. "What are your weaknesses?" might be a hideous question, but you should avoid wheeling out the clichéd answer, "I'm a perfectionist." Instead, turn a negative into a positive. Career coach Karen Gee suggests saying something like, "A few months ago I realized I needed to take a refresher course in French. So I started an advanced seminar and now speak as well as I did when I spent a semester in college in Paris."

questions you should have answers for

- Why do you think you would be well-suited to the job?

- What relevant experience do you have?

- Is there anything you think you might struggle with?

- How would you be able to contribute to the position?

- Why did you leave your last job?

- What has been your biggest challenge to date?

- What salary would you expect to receive?

- Are you happy to work overtime when required?

Dress to impress

Everyone knows that it only takes 30 seconds to size someone up. To make sure you get beyond the half a minute mark, do a "test run" the day before to ensure you turn up at your interview looking your best. This way you will know where you are going and how long it will take to get there. You don't want to ruin your outfit by running from the train station to make your 10 A.M. appointment. Plan to arrive 20 minutes early and sit in a café, relaxing and pulling your thoughts together.

When selecting what to wear, consider how other people in the industry dress. Is it an image-conscious position? If so, how you dress that day will play a significant part in your interview process. Even if the industry is quite casual, you should wear an ensemble a notch above what would be required to show that you are serious about the position. Decide what you are going to wear the night before, try it all on together, and have it laid out and ready. Pick something you feel good in, but that is still comfortable. Be clean and coiffed—hair pulled back into a simple mid-level ponytail and natural make-up.

what to ask?

- A detailed description of what the job involves

- The salary

- The hours

- Vacation time

- Health benefits

- Promotion prospects

- Will you be offered any training?

- What other company benefits are offerred—in-house cafeteria, retirement fund, affiliate discounts (gyms, sporting events, theater tickets, travel)?

Network like a pro

To make it to the top you will need to find yourself some key contacts. You probably don't want to work the door on a club to meet big TV honchos, but the principle is the same. Networking is just another word for having good people skills, helping them out, being helped by others, and making use of the knowledge and insights of those around you to keep yourself informed.

Most successful people are extremely busy, but if you ask a mutual friend, an acquaintance, or an old boss to put a word in on your behalf, a potential contact is more likely to respond. Be clear about why you would like to meet them and have a specific purpose in mind, whether it is to find out more about their organization or to ask for their advice. Suggest 20 minutes as a possible time frame; any longer would be seen as demanding. Most importantly, do everything you can to make it face to face— maybe they could slip out of the office quickly for a coffee or perhaps you could visit their office. Meeting in person will make sure you are remembered for a lot longer. Plan what you want to ask, don't be over-formal, but be clear about how you think they could help and whether they can suggest anyone else worth speaking to. By doing this you have already created a few more contacts. Avoid making a plea for a job and make it clear that you are only after expertise. Aim to interest people in who you are and what you can do, rather than trying to blatantly sell yourself. And even if you get nothing from the exchange, make sure you send a thank-you note.

Whether it's a sales conference or simply a company social, the very thought of a networking event may make you shudder. In a situation like this it's important to always remember that networking is about business, not making friends. Focus on who you need to talk to and what they can offer you. Try to consider the long-term; they might not be able to help with something you are working on right now, but it could be well worth establishing a relationship which might come in handy a few years down the line. And don't forget networking is a two-way thing—what do you have to offer them? At all times be professional, sell yourself, and focus on the task at hand, making connections.

Don't hang up your handbag

Never give up. Hardly anyone gets the first job they go for. Every rejection should make you more determined. See it as a valuable character building process—you have gained interview experience, learned about research and preparation, and now you are ready to sock it to them next time round. Although successful people appear to fly to the top, it is only because they don't talk about the jobs they didn't get. Would you advertise your failures?

> **"When I moved to the city, I needed to get a job quickly to keep the cash coming in before I could look for something more interesting. I dressed-up, put a stash of resumes in my bag and walked up and down the local streets, dropping in to every restaurant and café that I liked the look of. Each time I asked to see the manager, explained that I had waitressing experience and gave them my resume. I got a job that day."**
> **MOLLY, 21**

HOW TO BE A PEOPLE MAGNET

Find a friend (or two)

What could be more important than a stellar group of friends? Like Carrie Bradshaw, your trusted inner circle will be your greatest asset. They will whisk you off for a night of cocktails when your boss or boyfriend has been a nightmare and will get up at 6 A.M. to stand in line for a fabulous sample sale with you. But how do you actually begin to make friends and where will you ever find these soulmates?

There's no denying it, moving to a big city and leaving your familiar gang behind is tough. Suddenly all your free time is one big void and you wonder what on earth you're going to do on the weekend. You feel grateful when someone on a park bench starts chatting with you or a shop assistant gives you a warm smile. Take heart, it's normal to feel this way when you move somewhere new. You probably want to spend every night calling or emailing your friends back home, but that's not going to help. Right now you need to work on building up a social life here in the big city.

So, what kind of friend are you looking for? Someone to go to the gym with, a buddy who

where to find a friend

- Common interest groups

- Work

- Through friends of friends, family friends, roommate's friends, work friends

- Neighbors

- Gym

- Nightclasses

- Church

- Sports teams

likes classical music, or a wild all-hours-party kind of friend? Chances are, you won't find everything you want in just one person, so make sure you spread your social network from one end of the subway line to the other. Different pals are for different occasions, although don't ever relegate someone to just one activity or day of the week.

Although you might know what you want in a friend, it's not much use if you haven't met anyone yet. So how do you find a cluster of buddies, short of introducing yourself to random strangers as "friendless and pathetic"?

How to meet people

Be realistic. When you left college or whenever you leave a job you have heaps of friends, and it's easy to forget that you didn't know a soul when you first started. The same is true when you move to a new city. It takes time to meet people, but once you do, your social circle will snowball. It all begins with confidence—if you feel good about yourself you will be attractive to other people. After all, would you rather talk to the girl in the corner who's meticulously peeling the label off her beer bottle at a party, or the person who is telling a story to a group of laughing buddies? To find that kind of confidence, you need to draw on all the good things people have said to you. Store away every compliment and when you are feeling a bit insecure, remind yourself of it.

Just like dating, you won't hook up with anyone unless you put yourself out there, so make the most of every opportunity. If you are invited to a party through someone at work, go. Even if you only know the host. When you are feeling uncomfortable and a bit out of place, tell yourself that you don't have to stay all night, you can just speak to a couple of people and see how the evening turns out. If you are invited to a show or someone's opening and it's not something that you're really interested in, go along just this once or suggest an alternative.

Consider making friends a bit like networking for your job. Work the room at parties and events. Introduce yourself or take on a task where you can speak to a lot of people, such as handing round the chips and dip, or filling people's drinks. You are certain to strike up an interesting conversation. At the very least, you will certainly learn a whole lot of names. Then later in the evening people will see you, introduce you to the people they are speaking to, and you can take up some of those interesting conversations again.

Friendship involves a bit of give and take, and unless you are willing to invest a little at this stage, it will be tricky to meet anyone. There is no point sitting at home and complaining that you are lonely if you won't make an effort to get out there. However, once you have made a couple of friends, it won't be very long before they start introducing you to their friends . . . and soon you'll have your choice of partners-in-crime and more invites than you know what to do with.

Where to find friends

There are plenty of places where you can meet new people. Just think back to all your friends at home and how you crossed their paths—this alone should give you an idea of how to meet new people. An obvious one is the workplace. What are your interests outside of work? Love animals? Want to train for a marathon? Think you should be saving the world? Start looking online or in the local papers for a group or organization you can join. Perhaps you'd rather play soccer or volleyball so you're instantly part of a team, people will rely on you, and you'll have regular games to attend. Language classes, photography classes, dance classes . . . any nightclasses are a good way of meeting people with the same interests.

On the Internet there are a number of friendship sites where you can meet people with similar interests and many dating sites have sections for finding friends too. Don't be afraid to try them out. Approach developing the ideal social circle with the same kind of determination that you have applied to job hunting. Chat with friends of roommates, friends of coworkers, and friends of any family you might

quick fix It's 8.30 P.M. on a Saturday night and you have nothing planned. You can't face another night of stupid Hollywood movies that don't resemble your life at all, and you're feeling thoroughly depressed. Now's the time to act. Ask your roommate if you can tag along with whatever she's doing; there's no point being proud. Text the friends you have and ask what they're up to. Got an offer? Take it—even if it isn't exactly how you'd choose to spend a Saturday, just get out into the world.

> "When I moved, a friend gave me a number of a friend of theirs in the city. For the first few weeks I left it at the back of my diary because I wouldn't normally call a random stranger, but one day I figured I had nothing to lose and just got on the phone. I'm so glad I did because it totally expanded my social circle. Funnily enough I got on really well with her group of her friends and hang out with them most weekends now.
>
> **POPPY, 23**

have in the area. You might not click with your cousin, but you could have a lot in common with one of her friends.

The most important thing is to be proactive. As soon as you know a few people, throw a party and tell them to bring all their friends along too. Make an invitation like a chain letter. Send each guest two letters to send to two friends. Invite your next-door neighbors too. After the night, ask smaller groups over for dinner. If making small talk with strangers isn't something you enjoy, practice! Think of a few fun questions to ask people, so that you are not immediately heading for "Have you seen any good movies lately?" Ask questions such as: "Where is the one place in the world you want to visit?", or "What present did you never get for your birthday when you were a kid?", or even "What vegetables do you avoid now that your parents are no longer feeding you?"

At times like this you have to be brave, take opportunities, and meet up with people you hardly know. If you take advantage of being out of your comfort zone to experience new things, you might even find yourself making friends that you wouldn't have dreamed of back home. Remember, you are changing now that you live in the city, try new things and be open-minded. And when you meet someone you really like, don't hesitate to call them and initiate plans.

Where do you find lifelong friends?

You could shave all your hair off, streak on national TV, or start dating your father's best friend, and they would still be there for you. She laughs at the same silly things and you know exactly what gets each other's goat. But where do you find friendships like that? All over the place, actually. From the subway to your sandwich shop, there will be like-minded people who have the potential to become lifelong friends.

To make the transition from acquaintance to soulmate you will have to invest in some serious time together. This means that chilling with a pal on a Tuesday night, painting your toes together, and talking with great sincerity about the characters on your favorite TV show is time well spent. As is emailing her when you should be working, texting her from the bathroom when you're on a date, and rushing round to her place with a stash of magazines when she's got the flu.

The best friends challenge you and your opinions, inspire you to greater heights, support you in bad times, and love you despite your faults. They don't make you feel guilty on a regular basis or betray your trust. These friendships are worth working on and putting effort in, because they will last a lifetime.

Friendships falter

Inevitably things will happen which seem destined to break up your friendship. Every person is an individual, we all have different perspectives, and you can't expect to control or predict anyone else's behavior. If that were possible, it would be a very dull kind of friendship. Sadly, however much someone means to you and however much you know they care, there will be times when they screw up.

Perhaps he pulls out of your long-planned vacation because he met some new guy. Maybe she loses the tickets you bought for a Bjork concert. Or she lets it slip to a colleague that you've got a secret crush on your boss. The first thing to remember is that something like this is normally a genuine mistake. If your friend is truly sorry, you are still allowed to be upset, but is it worth losing an entire friendship over? Be careful not to blow things out of proportion. Do express your hurt or disappointment, explain you need a cooling down time, and try to be gracious when she apologizes. Remember, it is never easy to keep saying sorry, even when you know you are entirely in the wrong.

When you screw up

She insisted you borrow her favorite top, you knew it was a bad idea, and then you spilt red wine down it. You can't afford to buy her another one and you haven't spoken for a week. Situations like these are horrible, but there is no point running away from them.

When you have done something wrong, you need to take a deep breath and admit it. Explain what happened, acknowledge how upset she must be feeling, and offer a cocktail-flavored olive branch. It is not something that you are likely to enjoy doing, but if you are in the wrong then it is simply something you have to do. Afterwards, give her space to chill out and get over what has happened. If she still won't talk to you, send her a box of chocolates or some flowers, and wait for the phone to ring.

Are you a good friend?

If a friendship is to last, you need to be more than just a fun person to hang out with. Do you listen to a friend's grumbles, even when you have heard them all before? Do you call when you know that she is down? Do you keep her secrets and forget her mistakes? If so, then you are a great pal.

Still not sure where you sit in the friendship stakes? Talk to your friends back home and ask them if there is anything they wish was different about you. Warn them to be gentle. Criticism, however constructive, is always hard to take! And never ever consider doing this after a few bottles of Merlot.

You have to understand that in any relationship, romantic or not, there will be times when things go awry. Misunderstandings, disagreements, and general screw-ups will inevitably get in the way at some point. But how these are handled and whether your friend runs or faces them will reveal what kind of friend he or she is. If she helps you stagger home on your stiletto heels at 9 P.M. when you have underestimated the effect of five Vodkatinis on an empty stomach, then she is a true friend. If he accompanies you fifty miles out of the city to visit a sick relative who stresses you out, he should score high on the true buddy chart. Pals like these will always stick by you, whether you live in the hippest zipcode or in the outskirts of suburbia.

If friendship is true, it should be a two-way thing. Don't swamp him or her with phone calls, texts, and emails. This behavior exudes desperation. In the same way, don't expect them to fill every area of your life. Be happy doing things alone, with different friends, and in new groups. To avoid major damage, there should be a few unspoken ground rules. If a friend needs to borrow money, only lend it if you are happy not to get it back. If she asks whether you've noticed she's carrying extra pounds or if she made a fool of herself in front of some guy, then she doesn't need you confirming the fact to make her feel even worse.

Finally, be generous and forgiving. So your buddy is never on time. In that case, you should learn to turn up 15 minutes late too, or ask him to meet 15 minutes before you plan to get there. If a girlfriend steals your style or starts to wear her hair like yours, try to be flattered rather than frustrated. Little idiosyncrasies can make or break a friendship, try to view them as endearing and search for the little side steps that make them less irritating. Because rest assured, you will have some "endearing" habits of your own to which you're equally oblivious.

It is possible to be good at friendship and socializing but it is much harder to be a good friend. Friendships are relationships that can withstand catty fights, long distances, and months of not being in touch or hanging out. The biggest killer of friendship, however, is neglect. A good friend is attentive and involved, even when life takes off and pulls you in every direction. Don't take your friends for granted and make time to spoil them a little. Send a cute text message to her when she has a job interview, find just the right gift for his birthday, or make a personal gesture when she is least expecting it.

quick fix You haven't seen a close friend in a while and you are starting to feel like you are losing touch with her. Give her a call and find out what she has been doing recently. Make an effort to support her and celebrate her talents. Go and watch her soccer game or meet her for a picnic in a local park. Make an effort and your friendship will get back on track.

Friends in season

City or small town, friendships always go through ebbs and flows. So she is working all hours, while you care more about making the most of your weekend. Don't write off your relationship and definitely don't criticize her to your other friends. Keep in touch and find things that you both still enjoy doing, such as going for dinner at the new Vietnamese restaurant downtown. Six months later you will probably look back and wonder why you ever questioned your friendship.

Just because you don't speak to someone for a few weeks doesn't mean that you don't have anything in common. Some friends are twice a week buddies, while others are good for meeting up with every few months.

"Friends forever" is perhaps no longer true as you leave school or college. As your life changes, so will your networks as you make new friends in each phase. It's just the same when you start meeting new people after you've been in the city a while. Suddenly there are more demands on your time and it's not so easy to fit everyone in. Perhaps you haven't seen someone in ages, but now you're in the same area it will be easy to hook up. Just give them a ring, life takes us off on tangents sometimes and if you were solid friends in the first place it will be easy to pick up where you left off, however many months or years have passed. As you move apartments or jobs, friends often fall by the wayside as you meet new ones.

Don't be afraid to let go. This ebb and flow is a positive process because the friends who stick will have stood the test of time—you will be close because you genuinely enjoy each other and have something in common, other than nothing to do on a Saturday night. While phasing someone out of your life can seem a bit wrong and hurtful, it can be even worse just to pretend to be someone's friend. Cutting ties and moving on will be healthier for both of you in the long run.

CITY SLICK

The glamorous life

It's essential that a girl about town knows how to make the metropolis work for her. Meeting the right people, finding the best places to go, and knowing exactly what to say will make all the difference between living a sensational lifestyle or one that sucks. From finding out about invite-only parties to talking your way into the hottest clubs, its time to learn how to get what you want, when you want it. And don't fret, money's not an issue for an "it" girl who knows how to walk the walk and talk the talk.

Clubbing

There are some great nightclubs in every city—the way to find the one for you is to start by figuring out what kind of music they play where. For example, if you want to hear hip hop, you'll be headed in a different direction from the girl who likes electronica or jazz. You are probably familiar with the DJs and artists who play the music that you like, and guess what? Now that you live in the big city, chances are you can see them live and in person. And if you go to these venues, you'll meet other people who like this music—a good pool of people for possible friendships or dates.

If you're not so particular about music, but rather want a fabulous venue with rooftop views or a plush, private interior that makes you feel like a movie star, make note of pictures you see in magazines like *InStyle*, *People* or *USWeekly* (and whatever the hippest magazines and newspapers are in your city—*Ocean Drive*, *New York*, *Los Angeles*, *Toronto Life*, *Vancouver Magazine*, *Georgia Straight* and so on). You can get into these clubs, but if you don't want to pay? Well, then read on.

Guest list savvy

So you imagine yourself getting out of a taxi in front of a club and going straight up to the velvet ropes, past all the wannabes waiting in line, and being ushered right in the door? It's actually not as hard as it seems, provided you do your homework first. Leave it until the actual night of the party and then it could prove to be a bit more tricky. Try doing a search on the Internet with the words "get me on the guest list" plus the name of your city or the name of the club. This should pull up sites for groups that can do exactly that—believe it or not, certain businesses, such as alcohol companies or record labels, pay people to make sure their events will always be packed to capacity. Many club websites also have sections dedicated to making sure you get exclusive entry.

Always make sure you look the part of the ultimate club girl. Be it hip hop hottie or mysterious Parisian beatnik, look as glamorous as humanly possible. Or maybe you're more unique—the kind of girl who sets trends and is constantly copied? Then play that role and stand out from the crowd. Simply the way you look may inspire

> One night I was desperate to get into the hottest club in town. It's always swimming with VIPs and I knew that unless I was on the guest list I didn't have a hope. Miraculously, I turned up at the same time as one of the big rap stars. I stuck right behind him as he strolled up to the door, smiled at the bouncers, and walked in like I was part of his entourage. Not only did I skip the line but I got in free too!
>
> **JILL, 22**

a club doorman to decide to let you in . . . or not. It is also much easier to get in somewhere if you are with a few other girls—just girls, no guys. Be charming—the snotty "don't you know who I am?" approach is ridiculous and even backfires on celebrities a lot of the time. Get yourself noticed in a tasteful, eye-catching way by the people who matter on the door.

Once you're in, get friendly with the DJs and the club owner. You might find yourself walking in for free in the future. The VIP area is a whole different ball game, and much harder to gain access to unless you're dating a VIP or really become a VIP yourself (which is always the goal, right?). In the meantime, start by making friends with the people who work in the club. If you like the club, you might even consider trying to get a job waitressing. Club staffs tend to be very close, bonded by late nights and crazy tales of club drama. Then you'll really be on the inside.

Fashion know-how

To look fabulous in the hottest spots in town, you need to find out where to shop and you'll need to refine your own personal "city" style. Designer sample sales are always worth checking out, though a designer item that was $1200 and is now "only" $600 on sale may not be such a "bargain." Besides, these sales really only happen in a few cities like New York, L.A. and maybe Miami. But department store seasonal sales can be pretty amazing too—you might expect to find a Marc Jacobs skirt on sale at Saks Fifth Avenue for less than it would be in a Marc Jacobs boutique. These seasonal sales tend to happen in January and July, so mark your calendar. The first day of the sale is a good time to scope out what's on offer, but it's worth waiting for the second or even third mark-down to get a real steal—just ask the sale staff when they think that will happen and keep checking in. And try to buy the classic items you find, not the trendy stuff that will look dated a year from now.

And don't forget everyone's favorite weekend destination: the outlet store. While outlet stores are usually located in the suburbs, many cities have designer discount stores like Daffy's, Century 21, or Filene's Basement that have some wonderful deals, especially if you are an odd size or tend to like the colors other people don't. Learn to love chartreuse or safety orange (both can be very chic . . . in limited quantities).

Another phenomenon in cities are consignment stores—boutiques where other women take designer clothes they bought and regretted. This provides a great opportunity for you—don't be surprised it you see a handbag you saw in *Vogue* or *Vanity Fair* in one of these shops for 30 percent of what it cost new. So what if it's a little worn-in? Well-made handbags and shoes get more handsome with wear.

Check out your city's Chinatown, Little Italy, or other ethnic neighborhoods. Items purchased here can look a lot like what designers are showing, and for good reason—they are often the original inspiration! Also, never rule out vintage or second-hand shops, especially those in wealthier areas. (Their cast-offs will generally be of better value.) Don't forget to forage in the flea markets. You can find the most amazing things amid the junk piles—you just have to develop your discerning eye.

When it comes to fashion, always mix it up a little. If you look at the style of someone like Gwen Stefani, Sarah Jessica Parker, or Chloë Sevigny, you'll see they combine clothes in unexpected ways—old and new, uptown and downtown, librarian and showgirl, cultural and athletic. Try to think outside of what fashion magazines say is really hot right now and build your look around the items you already have that fit you and look great. And never be afraid of holding on to items with sentimental value—your Mom's Pucci scarf or even your grandmother's jewelry—these are items that may be stylish as well as meaningful for you.

Basics vs. accessories

Personal style is more important than following trends. Fashion trends come and go. What you wear is an extension of your identity. You have to know your body and your face shape as well and feel good about them to dress well. But while you are dressing to look chic and stylish, make sure that you dress to please yourself. Think about what colors you like, the trousers that you are most comfortable in, and the fabric that feels the best on your skin. Extend your wardrobe based on the pieces that you love and wear the most, and don't be afraid to rethink your look from time to time and update it or mix it up with a different shirt or belt.

You can make inexpensive basics the foundation of your look and shop at popular chain stores without looking like every other girl about town. You can get some great pieces at good prices because lots of these stores have a sale rack all year round. They carry lots of mid-season items and they usually have discounts on certain current season items as part of a promotion. Don't be shy to enquire if anything is on sale, and always ask if there is a damaged rack. Chain stores, such as The Gap, Limited, Old Navy, H&M, Club Monaco, French Connection, and Banana Republic, often sell damaged items at marked-down prices. These are usually easy to repair or clean up if you go to a bit of effort. Just remember that you probably won't be able to return anything you buy from a sale or damaged rack.

Basics in black, such as a pencil skirt, a blazer, a nice pair of dress pants, and a turtleneck sweater from chain stores can be dressed up to look like a million bucks. Just be wary of the fact that these clothes aren't tailored as well as their more expensive counterparts and can be boxy or square—try things on and make sure they fit well and are flattering. Never be tempted by a bargain that doesn't suit you and avoid buying clothes that you don't need just because it is on sale.

You can pretty much get away with wearing anything off the rack if you invest in great finishing touches—such as a handbag, shoes, sunglasses, or a coat—that make an outfit look polished. If you have expensive shoes or a good coat or handbag, people will automatically assume that the whole outfit is designer. As you earn and save, these accessories are worth spending on. But again, think classic, not trendy—you're an adult now! Buy items like a Burberry trench or a Dolce & Gabanna black wool coat or Gucci black leather boots you might expect to keep and be wearing for a few years.

If you are tempted to get something really trendy and of the moment, you might as well get them from chain stores, where knock-off shapes and styles are much less expensive than the designer version. That way, in a few months when you're tired of this item, you won't have any problem passing it along to your favorite thrift store.

And to avoid spending too much money, be prepared when you shop. Take a clipping from a magazine or a newspaper ad with a picture of the item you are looking for with you. You could even phone in advance and ask the store to hold something. If you are buying an item to match another piece of your wardrobe, bring that piece along so that you know that you are making a great match. A truly stylish girl will have one outfit that works from head to toe each season.

quick fix You don't have a lot of spare cash after paying the bills each month and find yourself buying much of your wardrobe in the cheaper chainstores. You can still look great by taking care to iron your clothes. Cheap fabrics look much better ironed. You could also replace key features of pieces, such as the buttons on cardigans, to give the item a bit more style and a personal touch.

Clothes for cash

If you're broke but still want to shop, go online and sell some of your discards on eBay. As long as it's something in reasonable condition and has a recognizable label on it, chances are good someone will want it. $15 here, $30 there—it starts to add up. Just make sure you charge your buyers enough to cover eBay fees and shipping charges. eBay is also great for finding clothes and accessories at phenomenal prices. But before you start shopping on eBay, pick up all those clothes that have fallen off their hangers and been lying at the back of your closet for the last six months, and sell them.

It may seem like a pain in the ass at first, having to trudge to the post office to mail out your items, but as the money starts coming in, it will be worth it. And if you are really industrious, you could go to a designer outlet near you, buy a few pieces from there, and try to sell it "new with tags" on eBay to non-city dwelling girls who don't have as much access to discount designer goods. For example, let's say you bought a Gucci top at an outlet store for $60. List it on eBay for $120, and if it sells, you've made $60. If it doesn't, return it promptly—obviously, check to make sure the store will let you return it and most of them give you 10 to 30 days—and try another item. Check to see what is selling on eBay and for how much to make sure you are not over-charging and scaring-off buyers.

If you are not online at home, or don't want to rely on Internet cafés, consider getting a stall at a local flea market to sell some of your cast-offs. If you go to a market in the more suburban outskirts of your city, you could still sell discount designer goods. Otherwise, club together with a few friends or your roommates and have a yard sale. You may have to head home to your parent's place in order to find a yard if you live in an apartment or a really urban part of the city.

> After I saw the beautiful dress Charlize Theron wore to the Golden Globe Awards, I just had to have one. I did an Internet search on "ABS by Allen Schwartz" because I knew he would copy it and I found one very similar to it for about $200. ABS copies the best dresses from the award shows every year, so it's a great place to start looking when you can't afford the real thing.
>
> **PAMELA, 22**

Beauty on the cheap

Most beauty counters in department stores will happily give away samples of their products if you look like you might be persuaded to buy. "Use department stores to get your inspiration, but don't be tempted to buy big names like Guerlain or Chanel," says Mary Greenwell, a celebrity make-up artist who has worked with photographers such as Annie Leibowitz, Herb Ritts, and David Bailey, magazines such as *Vogue*, *Harpers Bazaar*, and *Elle*, and everyone from Cindy Crawford to Cate Blanchett and Gisele. "After you've checked out the department stores and tested which colors work for you, go to the drug stores and supermarkets to buy the cheaper alternative. These products can be just as good, but you need to do your research first to find the colors and textures that suit you best. Bourjois, L'Oreal, and Maybelline are all great cheap brands."

Keep an eye out for advertisements in newspapers and on public transport for special beauty promos with brands like Estée Lauder, where if you spend a certain amount they give away a free gift pack. As an insider tip, if you're living in a city with a warm climate, such as Sydney or New York, and really want your make-up to last, try keeping it in the fridge.

If you're desperate to buy the most expensive brands, even when you can't afford them, make sure you invest in refills. "Clinique, Bobby Brown, and Guerlain all do great refills," says Becci Field, Beauty Director at UK *Glamour* magazine. "They work out about a third cheaper than buying the whole product again." You probably won't have the cash to go down the designer make-up route but, "If you're going to invest in one product, make it a foundation," says Field. "Cheaper brands such as Rimmel and Max Factor do great mascaras. You can buy a quality blusher brush and then simply make sure your base is perfect."

If you're really broke, try combining your make-up to make the most of each item. "With 3-in-1s you can stain your lips, smear over your eyelids, and build up your cheeks all with one product. Mac also does good palettes where you can pick and mix and make your own colors," adds Field.

It's a good idea to bring along a stub of your favorite lipstick and other well-used items in your make-up bag when you are making new purchases. Then you won't buy exactly the same shade. Imagine the product in natural light, rather than under the glare of the in-store lighting, before you commit to any purchase.

When it comes to having your hair cut it's worth shopping around because it can be a pricey business. Some salons will cut your hair dry (so you don't have to pay for a wash), others will let you blow dry it yourself, which will save cash. Always check over the phone beforehand!

Otherwise, try visiting hairdressing schools, where you pay a fraction of the usual cost for a cut, and it's extremely cheap to get color, too. The students are watched very closely, but because they're new to it you will need to have plenty of time to spare. Try looking up big names such as the Vidal Sassoon School or Bumble & Bumble in the phone book. Otherwise, the training schools often advertise in free magazines that are distributed at subway stations.

KEEPING YOUR BALANCE

Make time for yourself

Living in the fast lane is a blast, but it can play havoc on your body and soul. You need to realize the importance of making room in your new exciting city life for downtime. As much as it seems like you should say yes to everything because it's all so fabulous, you can't let yourself get run down.

It's easy to get caught up in a whirlwind of metropolitan must-do's. Whether it's dashing straight from work to a party, from the gym to a dinner date, from shopping to drinks with the girls, it's tempting to never get off the merry-go-round of endless social activities. After all, you've been waiting your whole life to live in the city. But unless you take care of yourself, you'll quickly burn out. You won't feel well, look well, or perform well, so what's the point?

The city is now your home—trust that you can spend a night in once in a while and you won't miss anything that won't be there tomorrow. Think back to the time when you last felt most relaxed. Were you having an indulgent sleep-in on a Sunday morning? Were you sitting in the steam room after a hard workout? Or were you lying in the park reading a book? Whatever works for you, make sure you don't let it get squeezed out of your weekly routine.

quick fix Can't chill out in your apartment with all the sirens, car alarms, and street noise down below? Invest in a sleep machine. These wonder gadgets play about six different sounds, from a babbling brook to jungle fauna to rain on a windowpane. If these melodic riffs can't lull you into serenity, nothing will.

Schedule an appointment for relaxation every week—block out an hour or two and stick to it as you would any other appointment. That way you will have a chance to replenish your body so you look, feel, and function better all week. And even on a daily basis, think about when you can fit in 20 minutes of "me-time." Perhaps you always eat your lunch at your desk. If this is you, get outside and go for a walk or a drink in a near-by coffee shop. Sometimes doing things alone can be especially re-energizing, particularly if you are surrounded by people all day. Even extroverts need a bit of downtime just to have your own thoughts and a few moments of reflection.

Urban beauty tips

Unfortunately along with all the fantastic sights of the big city comes a heavy dose of pollution. Ultraviolet rays, which cause 80 percent of skin aging, combined with pollutants can really take a toll on your skin. But there are some simple things you should start doing religiously now in your early 20s. According to dermatologist Dr. Bradford Ketchum, creator of the SkinCare Lab in New York City, young women should wear a moisturizer everyday which includes a Sun Protection Factor (SPF) of at least 15—try for 30—and an antioxidant to help protect against the aging effects of sunlight and pollution. A moderately priced but excellent line is La Roche Posay, which includes an excellent sunscreen. Throw on a pair of shades and you'll provide double protection for the delicate skin around your eyes.

Often just the stress of living in a city can have a negative effect on your skin. Never be too tired to wash your face at the end of the day, as city pollutants will start to back-up your skin—and this means breakouts! You may even want to invest in some cleansing cloths. There are a number of good brands from Neutrogena to

Shiseido, and you can carry them in you purse for mid-day cleansing. Dr. Ketchum also recommends adding a mild alpha-hydroxy toner or gel to your routine to even out skin tone and help prevent breakouts. And if you do find yourself breaking out more in the city, Dr. Ketchum warns, "never pick at your skin! Some of the worst skin damage I have ever seen is from squeezing blemishes. Use an over the counter benzoyl peroxide product or a hydrocortisone cream to dry it up instead."

Keep a small make-up bag in your purse or at your desk at work—you never know when you might receive a last minute invite to dinner or to a show. Celebrity make-up artist and author Trish McEvoy says, "a few products can set you up for an evening out. Concealer is great for covering up anything you want to banish for the evening. A dusting of nude shimmer powder highlights cheekbones and eyes for an instant glow, while a black eye pencil lines eyes for high definition. Carry a richer, brighter or deeper toned lipstick or gloss and you are set!" Having these items on hand makes it easy to touch up your make-up and head straight out, rather than rushing home first. Some studies show that wearing foundation in the city actually creates a protective barrier for your skin, and women who wear foundation their whole lives can age better than those don't. Just be sure to use a high-quality foundation that looks natural and won't clog your pores. Also, use blotting papers to soak up extra oil instead of using powder to just cover up the shine.

If you find your hair, as well as your skin, gets dirty faster in the city, try wearing it up the first day you wash it. It will stay cleaner for longer by simply tying it back. Otherwise, invest in a can of dry shampoo or hair powder—Bumble & Bumble makes a great one in different hair color shades—and keep it in your bag. Pat it over greasy areas to dry them up, although be careful not to overdo it because you will end up with a strange chalky look. This tip is especially useful for rescuing a greasy fringe or for bleached blondes who only wash their hair once a week.

Beer belly alert!

Inevitably, life in a new city will involve tasting exotic new concoctions in downtown bars. Which is a marvelous thing, but you should watch how much you're drinking if you want your judgment to remain sound and your waistline to remain visible. Alcohol is full of empty calories, which means that not only do you fail to get any nutritional benefit from a drink, but booze also makes you hungry . . . leading you to consume twice as many calories.

The best thing you can do is to keep a check on exactly how much you're drinking. Alcohol also dries up your skin, so make sure you limit yourself and drink lots of water the rest of the time. If you start getting a "beer belly," exercise four times a week for one hour—which you should be doing anyway—and you should see and feel a change right away.

Choose the drinks you order carefully and you'll make life even easier. Vodka and gin have significantly less calories than a lot of drinks, especially if you combine them with seltzer and lemon or lime. Pick bottles of beer over pints, and small glasses of wine rather than large. If you start to feel a little tipsy, order a few soft drinks between alcoholic ones to keep a clear head.

quick fix In the noise and bustle of a busy bar it is very easy to lose sight of your jacket or bag, and for someone else to take them. If you know you're having a big night out, take a small bag that you can keep with you, don't take along anything you don't need, and keep your money out of sight.

Toxic recovery

While living in a big city means toxic weekends are par for the course, no one wants to scare the cat when they wake up in the morning. If you can remember to do a couple of things the night before, you will feel so much better the next day, and you will be ready for a Sunday of regaining your balance. First, after washing off your make-up, always remember to apply a moisturizer. It will make you feel more fresh-faced when you are facing the horrors of daylight. If it takes leaving your moisturizer under the covers before you go out so when you fall into bed you get a painful reminder, just do it. Also, have a glass or bottle of water lined up beside your bed and knock it back with a vitamin C supplement to kick-start the body's recovery process and combat all those vodkas. If you can, try and have some toast or cereal before you go to sleep.

When you wake up, down some more water (because you'll be dehydrated) and try to avoid fruit drinks. Your insides are acidic enough already thanks to the alcohol. After washing your face, take a chilled, damp washcloth from the fridge (if you were

quick fix Keep your hangover under control by drinking lots of water. Keep track of how many drinks you have that night by popping the cap, cork, or swizzle stick in your purse. Then when you get home, count how many you've had and that's how many glasses of water you have to get through. If you still feel nauseous and have a pounding headache the following morning, take an aspirin with a rehydrating sports drink.

super-prepared you would have put it there the night before, if not stick one in the freezer and it will cool extra fast) and press it over your face—this will help you wake up and will reduce puffiness. If you simply have to go out to buy a paper and a carton of milk and you still look like death, throw on a pair of sunglasses—the celebs do it all the time.

The morning after you've tied one on, you also need a substantial meal to pull you back. Avoid greasy foods—opt for protein—maybe an omelette with veggies and turkey sausage and lots and lots of water.

If you've made it through one hell of a hangover, Sunday night has rolled around, and you're dreading the week ahead, then it's time to indulge in a serious pampering session. Have a bath surrounded by candles, slather yourself down with some nice body lotion, prepare some hot tea, watch your favorite "pick-me-up" TV, and make it an early night.

Feel-good food

Eating well is fundamental to feeling and looking good. Make sure you take time to grab a bowl of cereal or fruit smoothie before you leave the house in the morning. The myth that only fat people skip breakfast actually has a lot of truth in it. If you munch on some food early you'll avoid eating muffins and croissants at your desk a few hours later. When you can, cook extra for dinner and take it in a tupperware container for lunch the next day. As much as possible, try to cook from scratch using fresh rather than frozen food. Keep it simple—plain fish fillets or chicken breasts are easy and delicious, especially if you invest in the miracle kitchen device of all time—a George Foreman Grill. Often healthy eating goes out the window when life picks up,

eat healthy

- Buy lean cuts of beef and pork.

- Chicken and turkey often cost less than other meats and contain less fat and fewer calories.

- Invest in a cheap blender to make fruit smoothies. It's much cheaper than buying them ready-made, and more fun than chomping on five Golden Delicious apples a day.

- Buy skim or 1 percent milk instead of full fat. Use evaporated milk instead of cream.

- Choose foods that are minimally processed. Pick fresh poultry or meat over those already seasoned; whole fresh potatoes over chips.

- Keep adding to your selection of spices, sauces, and dressings—they can make otherwise boring salads and meals seem new and exciting.

- If the first ingredient in a food or drink is sugar, corn syrup, or artificial sweetener, skip it—it has little nutritional value. Opt for nuts, fruit, or fresh fruit juices instead.

- And don't forget to buy breakfast foods—if you don't eat something in the morning, you're more likely to be desperate by lunch and eat something unhealthy.

so always try to keep some basic foods, like eggs, cheese, carrot sticks, apples, and peanut butter, in the fridge. Buying real food instead of processed foods can be expensive, but it's okay to buy good quality food—what could be more important than what you put inside your body? Wash vegetables well and peel them to reduce the chemicals and pesticides. With meat it's better to go organic so you don't eat the antibiotics fed to the animals. It's also not a bad idea to supplement your diet with a multi-vitamin with anti-oxidants—vitamins A, C, and E, zinc, and selenium—to help to counteract the effects of pollution.

When it comes to eating out, always order first. Studies have found that people are swayed by their friend's choices and that they end up eating more as a result. Drink plenty of water with your meal, and don't try to clear your plate. Stop when you're full! If you're going to a bash where there's likely to be tempting fried foods and lots of booze, have a healthy mini-meal beforehand so you're not desperately hungry. Most of all, plan ahead. Think about what you're doing, where you're going, and when you'll be able to eat. Carry some raw cashews or almonds in your purse in case you need a snack between meals. That way you won't be caught short in the starvation mode and be forced to resort to a burger joint.

If, despite all this, you've found you've put on a bit of weight, forget fad diets and don't even consider dangerous diet pills. There is only one simple formula that works—reduce the number of calories you're taking in and increase the number you're burning off—in other words eat less and exercise more. Ordering a grilled cheese sandwich and fries once a week is fine, it's daily bad habits that cause a problem. Try to go for the healthier option when you're out, swap cheese and mayonnaise for salsa or guacamole. And skip that frozen coffee drink every morning filled with 900 plus calories of milk and sugar! Try green tea or a latte with the milk but skip the sugar. Little changes make a lot of difference. It's a lot easier to not gain weight than it is to lose excess pounds once you're packing them.

Stress relief

Life might be more hectic living in a big city, and in some situations stress can be a helpful motivating force. But sometimes you can push yourself too hard. Far too many people place unrealistic demands on themselves. These could be as simple as not giving yourself enough time to get somewhere or setting very tight deadlines at work. Too many people see the journey to and from work as an inconvenience or are in such a rush to get home they make themselves (and those around them) miserable. Do those extra five minutes gained from rushing around and being grumpy really make that much of a difference?

If you are waiting for a train, remind yourself there will be another one soon. Or make sure you have a good book to read, so you won't feel like you're wasting time. Take time to just look around you, at the people, at the chaos and chuckle a little bit—you are officially now part of the rat race! Don't let it get to you.

Because of all this big city stress, it is essential that you find time to relax. Schedule a massage, take a yoga class, or even slip into a movie so you're forced to chill out for at least an hour a week. And never underestimate the importance of sleep, the most natural form of stress relief. The hours we spend snoozing replenish the body's supply of neuro-transmitters—hormones that help produce a positive mood. Experts recommend you get at least eight hours of shut-eye a night, so try to crash out and rise at the same time each day to keep your body in a rhythm. Ever noticed you find it difficult to fall asleep on a Sunday night? That's because the weekend's activities have disrupted your natural patterns.

Your health regime

In a lot of ways, it's actually easier to be healthy when you're living in the city. There are so many activities at your disposal such as gyms, bike and running paths, swimming pools, yoga centers, and dance classes. Plus they operate with more flexible opening hours. Some city gyms are open 24 hours a day, seven days a week, so you can workout whenever you feel like it (and maybe when the gym is less crowded). Then there are city marathons and charity runs, which give you something to aim for, are a great way to meet new friends or spend healthy time with old ones, and a give you a great sense of achievement when you complete them.

Where's the best place to exercise? Normally you would expect outdoors to be the perfect location for your lungs, but that's not necessarily the case in the city since the air contains concentrated toxins. To help reduce the ill effects of pollution, run or skate indoors, or away from built-up areas. If you must be outdoors in the city, avoid peak traffic times in the morning and sunny days because of increased smog—instead try to find a park. If possible, exercise near some water where the air will be a little bit cleaner. Try to breathe in through your nose, which will filter the air more effectively than breathing in through your mouth.

Getting sweaty

The thought of going to the gym might make you want to hibernate with a pile of magazines and a super-size bag of potato chips. If so, don't fret. Try to make exercise a natural part of your daily routine. This doesn't have to mean going to the gym and thrashing around with a crowd of other city dwellers; rather, take a walk to the supermarket instead of driving, or visit a friend on your mountain bike instead of taking the bus. It's a cheap way of travelling, avoids the stress of public transport, and gives you a workout too. Madonna is frequently photographed riding her bike around London, and when Kirsten Dunst was filming *Wimbledon*, she invested in a bike, complaining that taxi fares were too expensive.

The total bonus of living in a city is that many places are a walkable distance, and walking at a brisk pace is good for your heart, lungs, waistline, and spirit. It is often more direct and faster than other forms of transportation, too. If you can't walk, use the subway, which will keep you away from polluted roadsides and still give you a bit of exercise up and down the escalators and between platforms.

Twenty minutes or more of exercise a day will promote energy levels, make you feel positive, and ensure you have a strong immune system. Medically speaking, if you're not out of breath for 20–30 minutes at least three times a week, your fitness levels will be going backwards. This is easy to achieve if you walk to and from work; any kind of exercise counts.

It's good if you can find something that you really enjoy—Gwyneth Paltrow loves yoga and Catherine Zeta Jones is a golf devotee. So what activity or sport appeals to you? Exercise will not only keep you in shape, it will keep you happier. Exercise has been proven to release endorphins—happy hormones—which give you a buzz and can make you feel positive for the rest of the day.

If the gym is your thing, give yourself time to wind down in the sauna or steam room afterwards. Exercise followed by relaxation will even help you sleep better. It's all about keeping a regular, steady balance of working out, chilling out, and partying. If you hate walking, biking, and the treadmill, try the wide variety of classes offered by gyms these days. Yoga, pilates, or dance classes will be challenging and leave you feeling centered and calm. Many gyms in big cities also have swimming pools. This is a fantastic way to relax and exercise at the same time, clearing the city cares away as you thrash up and down the pool.

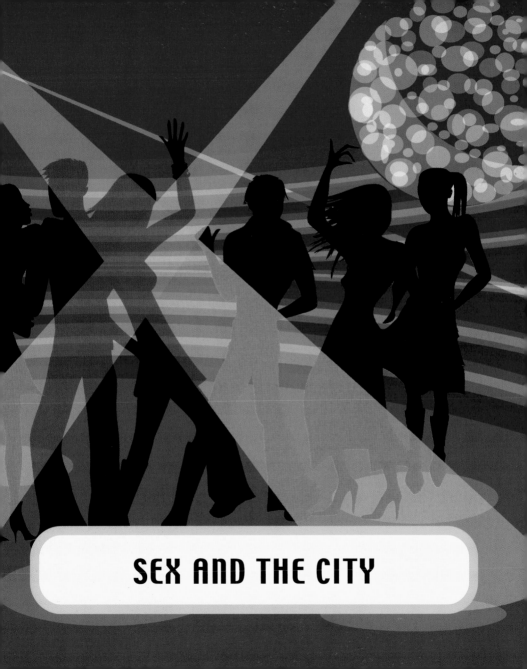

SEX AND THE CITY

The art of dating

Every city girl needs to know the rules of urban dating, from the bar right through to the bedroom. Add the fine art of flirting to your repertoire and you will be well on your way to becoming a true femme fatale. But do you know how to separate the losers from the keepers? Can you figure out who to pursue and who should be dropped like a hot potato?

Thankfully every city is packed with cute guys—from the slightly scruffy, artistic ones to the party-hard, athletic he-men, to the clean-cut business school types—so you won't ever be reduced to dating a friend's ex (a big no-no, ladies!). Gone are the days of begging pals to set you up with their brothers, or considering your high school sweetheart a second time around—now you can go out with whomever you like, wherever you like, and whenever you like.

So if a girl is looking to make headway in the dating scene, where should she go?

○ ○

ten places to meet guys

- At the gym
- At work
- At a friend's party
- Taking a class
- Doing volunteer work
- At a wedding
- At a café
- At the supermarket
- Out at a club or bar
- At an art gallery, museum, or exhibition

A popular central bar is a good first stop. Not sure which one to head for? Log onto a search engine and simply search "top bars" plus your city. It is bound to come up with plenty of suggestions, with reviews from recent publications, and a list of address and opening hours details. This will give you a good idea of where to start, and from there, make it a point to talk to cool-looking people and ask them for their recommendations.

It's easy to start talking to a guy as you order a drink and if he shows some potential, you can move onto a funky leather sofa for a more serious tête-à-tête. Nightclubs are also good for casual, get-to-know-you chatter, but a friend's (or a friend of a friend's) party is your best bet. Chances are the crowd at a private party will be more selective and the setting more intimate.

Dating services

If making the first move is completely foreign to you, it is worth checking out organized singles events. City newspapers advertise these parties and socials, and there is always more detail to be found on the Internet. There are hundreds of dating services out there that coordinate singles events and they really aren't so bad—at least you can assume that the guys who are at these parties are single and interested in having a girlfriend. Although dating services used to be for the socially unskilled, they have become increasingly trendy among city hipsters and make a lot of sense for people who are short on time. That said, the city is full of new, interesting men and you can meet a guy at every corner. There's only one method that's sure to not work—sitting at home. Just be open and aware of who is around, who is trying to get your attention, and how you can encourage them.

Internet dating is inexpensive and may provide a shortcut to meeting new people when you are new in town. Spring Street Networks run the Personals for publications as diverse as *The Boston Globe* and *JANE* magazine. They also link up with websites like gawker.com and nerve.com. The key to their success is the fun and irreverent questions they ask people who sign up—everything from "what's the worst lie you've ever told?" to "if you could be anywhere in the world right now, where would that be?" It's inexpensive, too—if you just want to post a profile so that men can respond to you, it's free. If you want to respond to other people's ads (so you get to do the choosing), it's about $25 for 20 credits (you use one each time you respond to someone's ad). It's even cheaper if you are brave and willing to let them publish your ad with a picture in one of their affiliate publications in your city. Then you can earn credits without paying, but be warned—though the stigma with personal ads is certainly less than it was, it's quite possible that your friends and coworkers will see your ad if it is published. Even people who aren't looking enjoy reading other people's profiles.

> "It sounds crazy, but I met my boyfriend through a website, nerve.com. My best friend had joined up and while she was reading through the profiles of eligible dudes, she came upon this guy Brian who she thought would be perfect for me. We had the same favorite book, we both loved surfing and we both said great passion was sexy, but great character was sexier. So she replied to his profile on my behalf and gave him my email. We started emailing, spoke on the phone and then finally had our first date. He's really grounded and yet, we're both dreamers too—it's great. We've been seeing each other ever since and its about three months now. Who knows where it will go, but it's so much fun. **ANNIKA, 23**"

There are hundreds of men to choose from in every online dating site, and it does get a bit overwhelming, especially when they are all answering the same questions. The upside is that so many of them seem cute and totally nice—like guys you might have met out anyway. But people do lie in their profiles—an article by Sari Botton that ran in the *New York Daily News* about the phenomenon of Internet dating reported that women most often lied about their weight and men about their age. Don't bother—be as honest as possible (after all, eventually, you will meet this person).

Once you start corresponding via email with someone, have a phone conversation with him before you agree to meet. You'd be surprised how much of a feel you can get for someone by their voice and the way they speak. If you still like the guy after a couple of phone chats, arrange to meet during the day or early evening in a public place for coffee. Don't meet in a bar for a drink at this stage. You want to stay in control and get to know him properly—and sober. Make sure you both have the opportunity to escape if it's not working out. Then, if you like each other after this meeting, commit to a full date.

Even if you have a few mediocre dates and don't meet someone you like using a dating service, take pride in the fact that you're practicing your dating skills and you're becoming more natural and relaxed about men in the process.

Does he have potential?

Are you looking for a fun affair with a guy? Or do you want to find someone who might turn into a boyfriend? Or maybe you're not sure—that's okay, too. Dating in the city can be complicated. So to start, just look for an attractive guy who knows how to have a good time, but who treats you with respect. Have fun with him, but pay attention to the details—is he well-mannered? Do you agree with his opinions (or at least respect them if they are different from yours)? Does he make you feel good about yourself by sincerely praising you? If so, he might be a keeper. At the very least, he should be someone you're not ashamed to introduce to your friends or your family, should the opportunity arise. He should be enthusiastic about showing you some of his favorite city spots, but be open to your ideas—even if you want to do the most obvious stuff at first (c'mon—you're new!). And if he has inside access through his work or social circle—like he knows when the latest club is about to open and has a friend who can get you tickets to a sold-out concert—well that's just a bonus, right?

Like any place, big or small, there will always be a few losers that you shouldn't allow to hang around, no matter how handsome they seem or what perks they can offer. If he already has a girlfriend, he gets drunk every time you see him, he lies, is pushy, loud, or critical of you, drop him faster than last season's Ugg boots.

The art of the lure

See that guy across the room? He looks decidedly sexy and definitely unattached. But how do you make him come over? Hold his gaze for a little longer than natural, and he will get the message. On the whole, men think that every woman is after them, even girls who are way out of their league, so he won't be surprised if you give him the gentle come-on. But how do you tell if he's interested in you? If he looks at you directly in the eye for more than a few seconds, he's interested. But how interested?

Get him to come over. How readily does he cross the room? Is he checking out other people as he walks toward you or is he maintaining eye contact all the way?

quick fix Can't shake off a guy who has bought you a drink? Buy him one back and gently explain that you want to be left alone now. Team up with a friend and head over to the other side of the bar. Don't look in his direction or give him any sense that you are aware of his existence. He should soon move on.

"I went to a speed-dating event in the city—this is when you show up and spend two minutes talking to each guy—sort of like musical chairs. I nearly backed out 10 minutes beforehand, but I was so glad I didn't. It was scary, but everyone else was a bit nervous too and I soon got into the swing of it. I met about 20 guys who ranged from great to geek, and I had a good laugh. A couple of dates came out of it, nothing serious, but enough to say I had a great time and would definitely do it again L I S A , 2 5"

When you start chatting, check out whether he starts imitating your behavior. Does he sip his drink when you do? Does he lean his head to one side at the same time as you? This is a sure sign he's in tune with you and wants to know you better.

Feed him tidbits of information about yourself, but keep the focus on him. What does he do? What is he into? Who are his friends? He'll have a good time talking about himself, then realize he knows next to nothing about you. Cue the first date.

First-date dramas

After a volley of witty banter, he suggests going for a drink. He is hotter than New York in August, so of course you agree, primarily because you can't wait to parade him in front of your friends. But where to go? First dates are much easier if you have something to focus on other than attempting to fill three hours with non-stop exchange. Suggest going to the races, an art exhibition, or a sports event. That way you will get to see him in a different context, and there is *always* something obvious to talk about if the conversation runs dry. A daytime meeting will also mean that you have the option to leave at any time without it being weird—bailing out on a date at 9 P.M. is always embarrassing. Plus there will probably be less alcohol involved, saving you from an attack of the guzzle-nerves and a morning of "I have a horrible feeling that I did something embarrassing . . . if only I could remember." As for the movies or theater— don't even consider it. These are hardly get-to-know-you environments.

Avoid the intensity of going for dinner or drinks; this date should be fun, not hard work. He knows as little about you as you do about him, and you don't want his first and lasting impression to be that you are either a boring person with nothing to

dating tips

Do give a guy a chance.

Do go somewhere relaxed, ideally a venue that creates conversation.

Do talk a little about yourself, such as your family, job, and aspirations.

Do ask him about his life.

Do have a good time.

Don't write him off because you hate his shoes. He can always get new ones.

Don't do dinner on a first date.

Don't start revealing your relationship history and philosophies on life.

Don't interrogate him about his ten-year life plan.

say or that you chatter endlessly about nothing. Unfortunately, both of these scenarios are possible if you're facing several hours of intense conversation with a relative stranger. Also, if you decide the whole thing is a mistake, there's nothing to take your mind off the bad date.

What to wear? Jeans with heels and a silk top show you have made an effort but haven't gone overboard. That way he won't feel like a fool if he turns up scrubbed or scruffy. Try to dress for the occasion. You don't want to overheat on the first date. There should be only one thing that causes your temperature to rise, and that should be the man you're with, right? Getting a little cold might be ideal, however, if you feel you want to cuddle-up to keep warm.

So it doesn't go as planned? Don't worry. If the exhibition finished last week, the sports event was rained out, or the queue for tickets stretched around the block, keep positive. You in a bad mood will only add to the problem. Sure it's a disappointment, but it's also a great way to see how your man behaves under pressure and how inventive he is when he's thinking on his feet. After all, if he's going to get stressed and grouchy about this, what will he be like when something really disappointing happens?

Turning a first date into a second

Things are going well on your first little venture together and you would love to do the same thing all over again next week. But how do you make sure he feels the same way? Well, you can't force him into liking you, but if you keep it fun and light, there is a good chance he will. Think about the dates who have made you feel good and how they managed to do that. He is bound to be nervous, so reassure him. Tell him you are having a good time and congratulate him for choosing such a great place.

Keep the conversation flirty and slightly provocative. This is a first date, remember. If there is going to be a second then you shouldn't be in any hurry to reveal your entire life story in one night. Chatting about your career, friends, films, books, and what you do on the weekend is a good way of creating two-way conversation. Avoid mentioning your ex, your mom, or your phobias. Think of a first date a little like a job interview. You want to sell yourself and you want to find out what he has to offer. Is he worth giving up your single life for? Gently sound him out without making it seem like a police interrogation.

Afterwards, send him a short text message or email to say you had a good time. Keep it brief, friendly, and reassuringly normal. If he gets back to you, bonus! If he doesn't, well at least you conducted yourself well and had a good time.

The unveiling

If he has jumped through all the hoops, ticked off all the boxes, and makes you laugh, day and night, it is time to introduce him to your friends. Don't make it an en-masse event, rather pick a couple of close friends and make them promise not to grill him or scare him away.

Choose a neutral place, like a café, and try not to expect too much from him first time round. Knowing that he is about to be paraded in front of a group of people whose opinions, for the moment, matter more than his, is bound to be a nerve-wracking prospect.

○ ○

inner circle access

Do warn your boyfriend beforehand about any high-maintenance friends.

Do make your friends swear not to grill him.

Do give him a decent amount of warning so he can get used to the idea.

Do remind him beforehand how much you like him.

Don't freak him out by revealing that your friends are dying to meet him.

Don't prep him on what he should and shouldn't say or wear.

Don't let him drink too much.

Don't try to introduce him to all your friends at once.

On the flip side, when he decides to introduce you to his friends, try to imagine they are simply a new crowd of people rather than a group you desperately want to impress. Remember he likes you, so they probably will too. Resist trying too hard. Don't join them in making fun of him and *never* flirt with his buddies—unless you want this to be the last time you see him. No amount of nerves can excuse such a social faux pas. If possible, try to find a night where a handful of his friends and a few of yours can all meet up at the same time. That should even out the pressure.

Their verdict

Of course you should listen to your friends' opinions. They know you well and may have a clearer perspective on your relationship because they are outside of it. However, don't let them judge your man based on one night. If they think he is fabulous, great. If they gave him the thumbs down, hear them out but do so with an objective mind. What are their concerns based on? It would be a dream if everyone you went out with could charm the pants off all your friends (not literally), but just as some friends of yours don't get along, some boyfriends and friends won't either. All you can do is keep "selling" one to the other and hope eventually they will see eye to eye, or at least learn how to keep the peace.

In the same way, if you can't stand some of your boyfriend's friends, try to keep it to yourself. He may have known them for years and recognize their faults, but shared history means they still hang out together and you should respect that. Moaning about his friends will simply put distance between the two of you. Try to accommodate his feelings. Only if their friendship gets in the way of your relationship should you express your feelings.

Spice up your sex life

When you're away from home in a new environment and surrounded by people who don't know you very well, it's easy to forget exactly who you are and what you do and don't want to do. Maybe your new city girlfriends are really daring and like having casual sex with strangers in hotel rooms, have a penchant for sex videos, or sing the praises of sex swings. Good for them! But remember that whatever you do and whatever you don't do is entirely your choice.

Sex is something that has to feel right, so never be pressured into falling into bed with someone. A one-night stand with a complete stranger in a town you barely know probably isn't the brightest idea. Listen to your instincts. If you have any reservations about the guy then pay serious attention to those feelings. If he's completely irresistible, can't you give him your number and meet him tomorrow night when you're not so tipsy? If you do decide to go for it, make sure your friends or roommates know where you've gone and of course, always use condoms. It might sound obvious now, but it's easy to forget in the heat of the moment. Even if you're on the pill, do you want to risk catching a grisly sexually transmitted disease? If you wake up with a thumping headache and realize you weren't careful, get yourself down to the local clinic ASAP!

If you're in a relationship, the chances are you've probably got a pretty good sex life already, but there is no harm in juicing it up a little. "Keep things steamy by emailing or text messaging him the first two sentences of a sexy fantasy, along with an instruction for him to send it back with the next two sentences added," suggests Tracey Cox, from BBC dating show *Would Like to Meet.* "Keep going back and forth with the game until you both come home to turn it into reality." All big cities boast a number of sex shops and there are some great sex toys outlets online, such as babesintoyland.com. It is worth dropping in, with your man by your side, to browse through what's on offer, even if you've got no cash to buy. Add sex games and toys whenever you want to keep things lively. And if your between-the-sheets action is starting to feel seriously humdrum, think about taking your naughty activities outside. Rooftop terraces, penthouse suites, and elevators provide the perfect place to make things a little risqué.

If you're scared about being seen, plan a bed picnic. You need champagne on ice, food you can eat with your fingers, such as chocolate covered strawberries, frozen grapes, fresh cherries, and food you can smear all over each other, such as honey, ice-cream, cream, and fudge sauce. Get an erotic book, earmark the pages you want to try or find the hot sections, and read them out to each other as foreplay.

How to ditch him

So it has been a couple of weeks, a couple of months, or even nearly a year. But it isn't working. It is obvious and it just needs someone brave enough to call time on the relationship. Don't shy away from facing the task just because you go to all the same places or know the same people. This city is big enough for the two of you. But you do need to talk, and soon. First, explain as kindly as you can why you don't think you should be together. Try to do it face-to-face, but somewhere public, like a park, would be ideal because you won't attract huge amounts of attention.

If it happens the other way round and he decides to ditch you, remember that he obviously didn't appreciate you and you do deserve to be truly adored. Book a facial, splurge on a sexy dress, and head toward the salon for some uplifting highlights. There is a whole lot more fun to be had in the city as a single lady. Next!

OVERCOMING OBSTACLES

Ups and downs

Annoying but true—for all the ups in life there are going to be a few downs. And when the going gets tough you need to know how to survive those pitfalls. Being dumped, falling out with your friends, missing your family, getting fired from a job . . . these are all normal growing pains. But how do you get through the tough patches with a smile on your face? It isn't always easy but it is possible. Never wallow, admit to your feelings, and start the recovery process.

Unlucky love

He says it's over. You knew your relationship wasn't perfect, but you weren't about to give up on it yet. He won't or can't give you a neat tidy reason why he feels this way. He simply just doesn't think it's working out. So suddenly, unexpectedly, you're single. And you're not so sure you want to be. What to do?

First thing is to accept that if it's over, it's over. No amount of undignified begging or wishful thinking will change that, and it will only make you feel worse in the long run. After you've spent a few hours in your room shedding some serious tears, call your friends, go for a coffee, or a walk in the park, and talk it through. Discuss all the reasons why you were wrong together. Think about all the things you can do now you're apart. Cry a little (or a lot).

After a few days you'll have to start thinking about how you're going to pick up your life again. Inevitably there's going to be a bit of a gap, so actively find ways to fill it. Have you always felt like learning Spanish? Wanted to go visit an old friend for a weekend? Now you can do exactly what you want whenever you want, without considering anyone else. You can be fabulously selfish and self-indulgent. Singledom is liberating if you approach it in the right way. Go to the movies on your own, do stuff on the spur of the moment, hang out with colleagues from work on a Friday night, find out what all the other single girls are up to. And keep reminding yourself of the fact that all the time you were with the wrong person, you couldn't meet the right one.

When Tom Cruise divorced Nicole Kidman in 2001 everyone thought her career would be over. In fact, Tom did her a big favor. She went on to become an Academy Award winning actress and proved all the critics wrong.

the best things about being single

- You can go out whenever you want, with whoever you want, without checking in with anyone.

- You have more time to see your friends and be a good friend.

- You have more time to invest in yourself—take a class, join a band, start painting, or write a short story.

- You get out more and stay in less.

- You have control over your own money, holidays, and major decisions.

- You can be as spontaneous as you like.

- Feel like kissing someone new? You can!

Loser boyfriend

Got a trashy boyfriend? He keeps saying he'll change but he never does? It's simple, get rid of him. You deserve the best, and if he can't give as good as he's getting then it's time you moved on. Spell out in simple terms exactly what's wrong, and say you're done. He won't be in a position to argue. Tell your friends you're going to do it so you can't back out at the last minute, and promise yourself the chance to see how life improves without him. If you don't, you're letting yourself down too.

Once it's over, look back and see if your relationship history follows a pattern. If

how to get over a man

• Delete his number from your phone along with any cute voicemails, text messages, or emails from him you've been saving.

• Put away any pictures you have of him.

• Change your bedroom around, or get new sheets and new curtains.

• Don't let yourself obsess about the good times you shared together.

• Take up something new—join a sports team, take a photography class, volunteer for your favorite cause.

• Catch up with old friends.

• Treat yourself—go on a trip to someplace you've always wanted to see.

• Don't worry about dating yet—give yourself a chance to breathe and heal.

so, there's no point beating yourself up about it, but it's important to be aware of what's going on so the bad boyfriend thing doesn't keep repeating itself. Look at J-Lo. She's not so good at picking winners. From P Diddy and his weapons charges to boozing, gambling Ben Affleck, she always seems to wind up with a loser. She might be one of the world's most desirable women, but even J-Lo has her man-issues. While you are single, think about the qualities you'd like a boyfriend to possess. And next time you meet someone, listen to your friends and your family early on. Sometimes they see the stuff you can't. And if you still keep making the same mistakes, seek out therapy.

Sex mistakes

It happens. It was never a good idea from the get go, and in the cold light of day it seems ten times worse. So you slept with your boss, colleague, or best friend—now what? It's not a scenario you may want to repeat, but you can hardly run away and pray never to bump into them again. The only way to deal with this awkward situation is to talk about it, however embarrassing or painful that might be. Email or text message the person to make initial contact. Suggest going for a coffee to talk it through and help get things back to normal as soon as possible. Make it clear from your message that it was a mistake and you don't expect anything to come of it. If they do, this will give them some breathing time to get used to the idea. Console yourself with the fact that everyone does stupid things—you weren't the first and won't be the last. And anyway, it takes two to tango. Which makes them just as dumb as you.

Whether you've slept with the wrong person or the right one, be sure you've taken precautions against a sexually transmitted disease (STD) or an unplanned pregnancy. If you've had unprotected sex or your condom broke, make sure you get yourself some emergency contraception ASAP. Either go to see your doctor, or go to a clinic to get the "morning-after pill." If your slip-up was within the past 72 hours, you still have time to take it. If a few weeks pass and you find out you are pregnant, it might feel like the world is caving in around you, but it's important you focus on your options—keeping the baby, adoption, or an abortion. If you find yourself pregnant it's important that whatever you choose to do, is your decision. You need to take control of the situation and figure out what you want. Talk to your friends, your family, the guy involved—anyone you trust, who you know loves and cares about you. Cities have clinics where you can get a free pregnancy test and confidential counseling. But terminating a pregnancy is not something you should go through alone, no matter what—be sure to confide in at least one trustworthy person to hold your hand through it all. And once you are out of crisis mode, think about future prevention. All sexually active women should talk to a doctor about safe sex and contraception as well as get an annual gynecological check-up. If you are having sex on a regular basis, you may want to consider taking the pill (there's even one that helps clear up your skin!) or going on the contraceptive patch. However, you should still use condoms to protect yourself from STDs.

quick fix If you notice any strange lumps, discharge, or itchiness, then find your nearest clinic and make an appointment. It's nothing to be ashamed of and the doctors and staff aren't there to judge you. Rest assured—they have seen much worse.

There is a whole army of ugly bugs just waiting to get into your pants—genital herpes, warts, gonorrhea, HIV, and hepatitis B, to name just a few. Chlamydia is the most common STD among young people. It's dangerous because you don't always know you've got it, and it can lead to infertility in women. The good news is that chlamydia is easily treated by antibiotics. The bad news is that chlamydia is not the only STD.

You can go to an STD clinic anywhere in the city, it doesn't have to be one near your home or work (if that makes you feel more comfortable), and you don't have to be referred by your doctor. When phoning to make an appointment, make sure you mention if you would prefer to see a male or female doctor, and if you are uninsured, be sure to ask how much it will cost. At some clinics, you can get free STD tests and treatment, so there is no excuse not to deal with it right away!

Drugs: the facts

Acid, crack, marijuana, ecstasy, speed—when you find yourself with new friends, going to an endless string of marvelous parties and fantastic clubs you might be tempted to try drugs. The best advice is: don't.

Taking illegal substances, whoever offers them to you, is never a bright idea. What starts as a just-for-fun indulgence can soon turn into a crippling habit that will destroy your health, your looks, your career, and quite possibly your future. This is not what you moved to the city to do—to crash and burn.

If you find yourself craving drugs and indulging once a month or more, be aware that you are heading for a serious problem that could take years of therapy and hundreds of thousands of dollars to overcome (rehab is expensive!). You'll also disappoint all the people who love and believe in you.

The best tip anyone can give you is simple. Don't hang out with people who into taking drugs. If you are not around drugs it is much harder for you to take them. There are plenty of other ways to enjoy yourself and make the most of the city. After all, if you're really having a good time, you don't need drugs. If you're just trying to stay awake a little later than usual, take a "disco nap" before you go out or get a strong coffee or energy drink, such as Red Bull. And don't be pressured into doing something you're not sure of. No one who is really cool will try to cajole you into doing something just because they are.

If you or one of your close friends develops a problem, there are hotlines (do a web search on "drug abuse hotline" plus the name of your city) that give advice and information to anyone who has questions about drugs. The hotline can also provide confidential counseling to anyone who thinks they might have a drug-related problem or is concerned about the effects of drugs.

Career casualty

So your job isn't going exactly the way you'd planned. Maybe you've been turned down for a promotion, or been told you really need to finesse your performance or face getting laid off. It's scary but this could be the defining moment you've been waiting for—do you really like your job and the company you work for and want to move up? Or do you want to move out? Either you commit 100 percent from now on or you make a sharp but graceful exit. Speak to your boss and find out exactly what the problem is, then you can plan ways to address it and improve your position. Even if you decide to move on from the company, it will be useful to know what areas your boss thinks you need to work on.

Don't be passive

You know where you want to go and what you want to achieve—this is why you moved to the city. But if things are harder than you expected, don't give up. At times like this you need to make use of every opportunity to improve and learn from your situation and make the most of every contact that comes your way. Mariah Carey was no fool at networking. Once upon a time she used to be an unknown backing singer for rhythm and blues artist, Brenda K. Starr. Once, at a party, Mariah asked Brenda to pass on her demo tape to Sony chief, Tommy Mottola. He was subsequently responsible for making Mariah the best-selling female artist of all time.

There's no point living in a big city if you don't take advantage of it. Without putting yourself out there and seizing every opportunity, you are doing yourself an injustice. So at every party, bar, dinner . . . think about the contacts you could make. Don't wait for people to discover you, because it won't ever happen, you have to get out there and show them what you've got.

Cash crisis

Memories of being in the black are practically non-existent. Being in the red has become a permanent state and you've hit the maximum on your credit limit. What to do?

Sit down and make a list of all your expenses. Include rent, food, travel, entertainment, the gym, and anything else that you spend on that you feel is good for you and want to keep. Then compare it to how much you're earning and work out the difference. Is it a plus or minus amount? If it's minus, go back to your list and make some cuts—even if something seems like an essential item, it's not essential anymore because you can't afford it. Either you get an extra job, a better-paid job, or you cut back. Don't even *think* about extending your debt by getting another credit card or a loan because you'll find yourself in a far worse situation a few months down the line.

There are ways of saving. Perhaps you could switch from your private gym to a YMCA? Or ditch your membership entirely and go jogging in the park instead? If you jog to work then you could save on travel costs too. Try making your lunch at home rather than buying it every day. All clothes shopping should come to a halt and maybe you should consider selling anything you regret buying in a consignment shop—or remember eBay!

Start limiting those drinks at happy hour! Are your friends earning a lot more money than you? If so, you can't expect to keep up with their lifestyle and you'll have to explain that to them too.

Be creative about it. Could you get the bus to work instead of the train? It normally takes a little longer but it's nearly always cheaper. How about saving on rent by adding a roommate? If you can't bear the thought of that, try moving further out of the city where space will be cheaper. Cook with your roommates; it will cost less than making food on your own.

quick fix Everyone's handed you the cash to pay the dinner bill, but it's short. Instead of going through and working out who's paid what, just divide the amount that is missing by the number of people in the group and ask for that figure from each person. It's not your fault if people don't get their money right in the first place.

If you can't work out where your cash is going, keep a money diary for one month and list everything you've spent, including all the small purchases. That should help highlight where the hole in your purse is. If you are still struggling, work out how much you can afford to spend each week, take it out in cash on the Monday and don't use your card again until the next Monday—it's a hard way to learn how to make money last, but it works. The rule? If there's nothing left in your purse, you can't spend anything. For the ultimate in crisis control, cut your credit card in half. You can still use the number if you need an emergency plane ticket, but you can't pull it out in Versace ever again!

Missing friends and family

When you head off somewhere new to upgrade your life the social scene won't suddenly stop spinning back home. Friends will have a good time together whether you're there or not, and family members will get married and have babies. Shocking but true, life goes on without you. If you start feeling a few pangs, think about whether there are any relatives nearby who could become your surrogate family—even if it's just to stop by for the occasional Sunday meal and a bit of TLC. If there's no one nearby, a friend's mom is bound to be more than willing to adopt you! It's always good to bend the ear of an older person when you're feeling down.

It might be worth arranging a regular time to call your parents so you don't keep missing each other. Not much happens on a Monday night, so why not set it for then? And if it's not too far, try to get home every few months so you stay up on all the news and avoid feeling like you're losing touch. It's good to take a break from the city once in a while, but if that's impossible, don't beat yourself up about it.

Sometimes it's easier to express how you feel through letters, phone calls, instant messaging, and emails, and you might find you actually get closer to your family now that you don't take each other for granted.

Encourage your friends to come and stay as often as possible. Have an open house policy so even if they're coming to the city for a job interview or to see someone else, they know they can crash on your floor and you'll have a few hours to catch up with them. You may not be able to hang out as often as you once did, but be sure to make the most of the time you do have together. Find out everything— what they've been up to, how they feel about certain situations, what their plans are. And tell them what's really going on with you. You'll feel back in step with each other faster, even if you're not up on the minutiae of every day like you used to be.

Family fall-out

It might have been a couple of decades ago, but your parents's memories are perfectly intact about the day you learned to walk or the time you wet your bed. This is why it's going to be hard for them to believe that you are now an adult and can actually cope in the city all on your own. When you come back home for a visit and they ask if you've been wearing a coat or getting enough sleep, try not to roll your eyes at them. You might have been managing decisions, big and small, extremely well on your own for the last few months, but they don't know that. It might feel like they are trying to insult you, but to them it's like your first day at school all over again. How to deal?

First, do not protest too much! Rather, prove that you can take care of yourself. Become financially independent, talk about your ambitions and how you're going to

achieve them, and cook them dinner to prove that your culinary skills extend beyond mac' and cheese. For you this independence thing is fun and exciting; for them it's scary. So keep your folks in touch with what's going on in your life, call regularly, go visit when you can, and gently break those apron strings bit by bit.

Or maybe your parents really are monsters and you're glad to finally be out from under them. Fine. But eventually, you will have to deal with them or the effect they have had on you. Don't be too embarrassed about it. Everyone has parent troubles of some kind.

Making time for what matters

If there is a milestone event like a wedding, funeral, or birth, do everything you can to get back to your hometown for it. You may regret if you don't. If it's impossible, ask for a copy of the wedding video, beg for pictures of the newborn to be emailed as soon as possible, and send flowers for the funeral so you have been part of it in some small way.

When actress Carmen Electra was 25 she lost her mother and sister within two horrific weeks. She'd just landed a job on MTV's *Singled Out* when her mom was diagnosed with a major brain tumor. Carmen flew home straight away, her mom had surgery, and then her sister died of a heart attack in her sleep.

Interestingly, Carmen says it was easier to cope with the trauma because she didn't live in her hometown anymore. "Everyone else had to deal with it; I just got on a plane and told myself nothing happened." When something terrible happens, it's hard to know how to handle it. Carmen cried her eyes out, wrote poems, read self-help books, and eventually realized that in order to heal, she would have to deal with her emotions. She forced herself to look at a picture of her mom and remember how she used to be. Carmen said, "Once you let yourself feel the pain it starts to go away." She cut everyone out her life who didn't support her in getting better, went to the gym, took long candle-lit baths, and started therapy. Everyone finds their own way of getting over a tragedy, and it's important that if something terrible happens to you, you look for what's going to help you get through it instead of letting your feelings get bottled up.

Backfires

You thought it was a good idea. You assumed everyone else would think so too. You expected it to go down well. But it didn't. And now you're holed up at home mortified to go out, afraid what people will say, and seriously considering moving to Mongolia.

Whether you just starred in your first play and it sucked, or you belted out a song at a band audition and sounded tone deaf—you deeply regret it now. But hey, it happened. And everyone's dropped a bomb or done something dumb at some time. You are definitely not alone.

Janet Jackson obviously thought it was a great idea for Justin Timberlake to "accidentally" rip open her costume and reveal her right boob to the whole of America at the Superbowl. Millions of parents watching with their kids weren't impressed. How did Janet handle it? She went on TV and did a spoof of the whole event. That's exactly what you have to do when something seriously backfires. Laugh along and everyone will forgive you. Then pick yourself up and don't do it again.

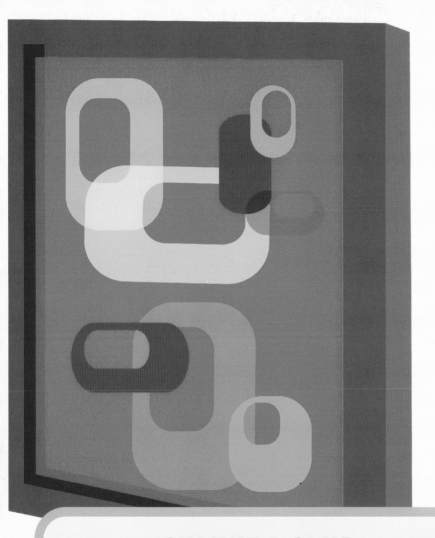

CULTURE CLUB

Places to be

Chances are, the minute you hit the big city you'll be thrown by all the zillions of things going on. Often there's so much going on it's difficult to work out where to go and what to see first, especially when posters, fliers, newspapers, TV, and magazines (not to mention friends) are screaming at you about the latest must-see person, place, or thing. If you've come from a small town where the local movie theater only showed one film for a month, to a metropolis where there are 20 multiplexes, it is bound to be a shock to the senses. But embrace it. This is the big city. It's the best possible place to be as young person—the world is at your feet. To find out what's going on, get on the Internet and look up citysearch.com or buy a copy of a local listings magazine (for New Yorkers—*Time Out New York*). This should be the first step to helping you figure out what's going on and what you want to check out first.

Tourist attractions

These places attract large crowds for a reason—Disneyland, Fisherman's Wharf, the Empire State Building. Some you have to pay for, some you don't, but they're all worth a look. Don't be afraid to buy a guidebook to your own city—a secondhand bookstore should have last year's edition of a *Fodor's* or a *Time Out* guide on sale for a few bucks. And now you're in the city, friends will come visit more than you realize, so take a bit of time to get up on all the sites so you can show them round.

To become familiar with a specific section of the city, definitely walk the streets—that's the best way to figure out what's really going on. Don't be shy—dip into interesting shops and restaurants, even if you can't buy anything. Just say you're looking around.

Taking a trip on the water can be a fun way to see the city in a different light. Taking a bus tour might seem be a bit crazy, but much like buying a guide book, it will help you get your bearings when you've first moved to a new place. If you are looking for something a bit more gothic, city cemeteries can be fascinating places. Just be sure to go when they are officially open.

Why not pop into a famous church, mosque, or synagogue? Look out for other historic buildings. Maybe you've read books that were set in your city in the past that detailed a certain cultural area or historical figure. Why not walk or drive around and see if you can find any of the old landmarks or sites from the story? You may be shocked by the ravages of time or thrilled by modern development, but either way you'll get a dynamic history lesson in the process.

Theater, art, poetry, and dance

When the theater is on your doorstep, it's criminal not to take advantage of it. Thousands of people travel miles to see Broadway shows, so whether it's a musical, serious drama, or Shakespeare in the Park, catch at least one of them while you can. Most cities sell off cheap tickets on the day of a performance. Check out a local listings guide. It may also be worth going directly to the theater or venue a couple of hours before show time to see if you can get any no-show seats. Even if not, what's a little detour in the big city on the off-chance of seeing something spectacular?

In most cities there are central booths and agencies that sell tickets for the major shows. Otherwise, look for shows happening in smaller theaters, in clubs, or at alternative art spaces.

In any major city, there are serious amounts of art to be soaked up, from edgy modern photographs to priceless thousand-year-old paintings. If you really don't know what you like, try a little of everything until you do. Many museums are free or discounted one night a week, and many art galleries are free and only charge extra for special exhibitions, so even if you think you're not a huge art enthusiast, it's always worth having a look. You might be surprised by what you see and by how relevant an art work can be to your life. Also, gallery strolls are a great date activity, giving you something to focus on, other than each other, while you gently reveal your likes and dislikes. And as a bonus, sometimes gallery openings provide free wine and cheese, and live music!

If poetry is your thing, with the number of aspiring poets in the city you'll have no trouble finding a café or art space with informal readings, or an open mike night. Poetry Slams, which resemble people performing live, spontaneous raps in head-to-head competition are giving poetry a major facelift. Again, don't turn your nose up at anything until you've checked it out. If you want to develop your own craft, hit the local bookstores for information about workshops and writing groups.

For opportunity to meet authors, browse the local listings and look out for posters in major bookstores, such as Borders and Barnes and Noble, or at universities and colleges. Many of these readings are free as they hope you'll come and be so inspired by the author, you'll buy his latest book. As for dance, once again you're in the right place. Ballet, contemporary, hip hop, or jazz, anything you're after will be available in abundance. And both performances and classes can be found at reasonable prices too.

Cinema

Blockbusters galore and art house indies too—in most cities there are movies showing every night of the week until the wee hours, and on weekends there's even a midnight show or two to be found. If a big movie is opening, you might want to call and book in advance on moviephone or fandango.com. Check your local newspaper for all the listings.

If you want to be the first to see something before all of your friends, go to your city's film festival, where you can watch a huge variety of movies before they come out in general release. It's very cool to recommend the lastest film having seen it before everyone else. IMAX cinemas are always worth a look too. The giant screens lend themselves to depictions of extreme sports like rock-climbing or deep-sea diving, so you take a virtual trip somewhere really exotic in just 90 minutes.

Otherwise, keep an eye out for second-run movie theaters, where they show films just a few weeks old at half price. And if you like things a bit wacky, look out for interactive movies like the *Sing-a-long-a Sound of Music* showings or midnight runs of *The Rocky Horror Picture Show*. You go watch the film, dress up, and sing along with all of the movie songs.

quick fix Your parents have descended on you for the weekend and you can't think what to do with them. Suggest a riverside or penthouse restaurant with a great view (and a hefty price tag!). They'll love it, and you'll get a fabulous free meal in a place you could never normally afford.

Bars and clubs

Whether you're after dance, techno, or a retro-80s night, your local listings magazine or website should have a club section to help direct you the best places to be seen in your city. The same goes for all the trendiest bars—they move on fast so it's best to check out any good listings source to find out where the scene is. Pay attention to bars owned by celebrities—they tend to attract others too. Don't spend your time in the city looking for famous people—your time will be much better spent becoming a VIP yourself! But every new experience is a chance to grow, so as we've been saying all along—try new things, have an open mind, figure out how everything works and how things are connected in your city. Develop your own likes and dislikes and opinions—this is what is going to make you stand out in any crowd.

Music

The biggest artists always tour through the most populated places; so now you live somewhere that's on the map, make sure you don't miss out. The majority of cities have a couple of places where the major stars perform. Check out concert listings or the back of newspapers for concert ads. Alternatively, go to a major ticket distributor, such as Teleticket online or to the website of the musician you'd like to see. You'll find out about scheduled shows and when new dates are added. There are always a few cool jazz spots to be found in a big city.

And while you've got the chance, why not check out a symphony or an opera? Most cities have an opera house and lots of the performances come with subtitles, so you should have a vague idea about what's going on. If you sit with the gods it shouldn't cost a fortune, and it's always worth going just to see the inside of these phenomenal buildings. And for the impoverished, there are always free music festivals and performances going on in the city in parks and other public spaces. Check the listings for these events too.

Restaurants

From sushi and burritos to Lebanese and Ethiopian, everything is on offer in the city, and you have to try it all . . . if only once. Remember that the key to being a city sophisticate is to be able to talk about what you like and don't like from experience. So be bold. Always ask the waiter or waitress to explain any terms or names on the menu you don't know, and if you're really stuck, ask them to recommend a dish to suit your taste. Most cities have really good guides to cheap eats, so you won't have to spend a fortune to explore these culinary niches, either.

Hotels

If you feel like soaking up a bit of the ambience, but can't afford a room, simply check out the bar in one of the city's hip hotels. For the cost of a drink, you'll get to indulge in some great people watching, and it's always fun trying to perfect that "dressed-down-rich" look and pretend you stay in these kind of places all the time.

It's a good idea to hotel hop with friends. It's not uncommon for single women in hotel bars to receive unwelcome attention. Also remember, this is not a nightclub; there may be strict dress and behavior codes. Have a good time but keep it cool.

Sports

From major league baseball to NFL football games to championship boxing matches to wrestling—the city provides unparalleled access to sporting events. It's a blast to check out some of the major sporting events. Even if you're not a huge fan, go along to soak up the atmosphere and find out what the obsession is all about. If you're more into alternative sporting events, check them out, too.

Parks

Many parks in big cities seem like cities unto themselves. People pushing baby strollers, or running with their headphones on, or napping on the lawn. Parks are great places to relax during the day and to meet people and expose yourself to free music or theater. It's likely you'll also be able to watch old men playing chess and hunky dudes having a basketball match. It's a fun and free way to spend a Sunday.

Markets and street fairs

Every city has some great markets and street fairs and they are fantastic places for picking up items with tremendous character at low cost. Listings magazines will usually alert you to the hours and location or you could do an Internet search on "flea markets" plus the name of your city. Even if you don't want to buy, there are some real characters to be found here and in good weather they are usually outdoors—so why not take a stroll? This can also be a fun date activity.

Armed with all the knowledge necessary to make the most of being young, hot, and in the city, the rest is now up to you.

And this is where the real fun begins. Hopefully, you'll fall in love . . . with your city. It's a wonderful feeling. You'll start becoming more yourself—the "it" girl you've always wanted to be. Sexy men will be easy to find—or to lose—and you'll know how to handle them and the growing pressures of your blossoming career.

You'll soon be on the fast-track to developing skills and contacts that will shape your bright future. When you're not entertaining out-of-town friends and showing them the sights, you'll be learning more about everything—art, music, food, and different cultures in the city or hanging out with your circle of friends at your favorite clubs, bars, and cafés. The people at your local deli and diner know your name—you've become a local. You're taking care of yourself so you won't get burnt out, you have found the best ways to chill and stay healthy, from eating organic to indulging in spa sessions. So, now's the time to stroll off into the city sunset and live all your dreams. The stage is set for your own amazing story to unfold.

RESOURCES

Chapter 1: Urban living

Find a place to live or a roommate
www.apartments.com
www.craigslist.org
www.flatster.net
www.movingcenter.com
www.roommates.com
www.roomster.net
Search: "Rental" plus name of your city

Tenant's rights and legal aid
www.lawyers.com
www.legal-database.com
www.rentlaw.com
www.tenant.net

Chapter 2: Street smarts

Public transportation
Los Angeles: www.mta.net
New York: www.mta.nyc.ny.us
San Francisco: www.sfmuni.com
Washington, D.C.: www.wmata.com
Montreal: www.stcum.qc.ca
Toronto: www.city.toronto.on.ca
Vancouver: www.translink.bc.ca

Find a doctor, dentist, or medical clinic
www.about.com/health
www.ama-assn.org
www.findadentist.com
www.webmd.com

Search: "Community health" plus name of your city

Chapter 3: Finding the perfect job

www.careerbuilder.com
www.jobshark.com
www.jonshark.ca
www.mediabistro.com
www.monster.com
www.monster.ca
www.nytimes.com/pages/jobs
www.workopolis.com
Search: "Jobs" plus name of your city

Chapter 4: How to be a people magnet

www.friendster.com
www.peoplefinders.com

Chapter 5: City slick

www.asos.com
www.clubzone.com
www.dailycandy.com
www.ebay.com
www.girlshop.com
www.ikea.com
www.style.com

Chapter 7: Sex and the city

personals.janemag.com
www.drdrew.com
www.epersonals.com
www.goaskalice.com
www.lavalife.com
www.timeoutny.com/getnaked

Chapter 8: Overcoming obstacles

American counseling association:
www.counseling.org
Canadian counseling association:
www.ccacc.ca
www.alcoholics-anonymous.org
www.drugfreeamerica.org
www.plannedparenthood.com
www.rapecrisis.com

Chapter 9: Culture club

www.canoe.ca/jam
www.citysearch.com
www.gawker.com
www.moviefone.com
www.ticketmaster.ca
www.ticketmaster.com
www.tkts.com
www.yahoo.ca
www.yahoo.com

ABOUT THE AUTHORS

Cathay Che is a writer and TV personality based in New York City. She has been a contributing editor at *Time Out New York* and she also writes for the *New York Post, InStyle, Glamour, In Touch, US Weekly, Details* and *Interview* magazines. Cathay regularly appears as a segment guest on a number of network television programs on CBS, CNN, MTV, and NBC. Since September 2001, she has traveled widely and, a surfing fanatic, prefers destinations with famous surf breaks.

Rachel Pask is a journalist living in London. After graduating from the University of Southampton, she worked as features writer at teen magazine *Bliss*. From there she moved onto help launch celebrity teen weekly *Sneak*, and then to the award-winning women's title *Glamour*, where she is now deputy features editor. This is Rachel's second book. Her first book was called *Panties*.

INDEX